Who Are You
When Nobody's
Looking?

Who Are You When Nobody's Looking?

MARC MARSAN

Illustrated by
Gary Kopervas

E L E M E N T

Boston, Massachusetts • Shaftesbury, Dorset
Melbourne, Victoria

Published in the USA in 1999 by
Element Books, Inc.
160 North Washington Street
Boston, MA 02114

Published in Great Britain in 1999 by
Element Books Limited
Shaftesbury, Dorset SP7 8BP

Published in Australia in 1999 by
Element Books Limited for
Penguin Australia Limited
487 Maroondah Highway, Ringwood, Victoria 3134

Library of Congress Cataloging-in-Publication Data
available.

Printed and bound in the United States by Courier

ISBN 1-86204-593-3

CONTENTS

Dedicated to Drew, Shane and YOU!

INTRODUCTION

A YOUNG man sat in a divorce court and listened as a judge described how he and his ex-wife would share joint custody of their three-year-old son.

The young man was angry, but not at his ex-wife, and not even at himself. He was angry at the judge and at the whole vast, impersonal legal system—furiously angry! It was maddening to hear this guy in a black robe telling him how often he could see his child. Had the legal system ever fed oatmeal to his son? Had the system ever tucked the boy into bed or taken him to the playground? Yet here was the judge talking about visitation rights and support payments.

It didn't seem real. But it *was* real.

Suddenly the feeling of anger transformed itself into utter helplessness. The young man wondered how he could ever again meet the responsibility of caring for a child, even on alternate weekends. It seemed beyond him now. He even felt physically small, like a child himself, like an infant being told what he could do and couldn't do.

He had been angry at the judge, had hated listening to his voice, but now he wanted the judge to keep on talking for as long as possible. As long as the judge droned on, the young man would not have to do anything except just sit there, and sitting there was the most he felt he'd ever be able to do.

But then the judge was finished. The hearing was over. Everyone was standing up. With the weird sense of distance from yourself that kicks in at such moments, the young man felt himself getting to his feet. All around him was a new, strange and overwhelming reality. He knew this was supposed to be his life, but he didn't recognize it at all.

• • •

That guy in the courtroom was *moi*, of course—and that was one of the most painful moments of my life. But today I treasure the memory.

Treasure the memory?

"But why? Why?" I hear you asking.

I'll tell you why . . . in a moment. But first, I want to emphasize that this book is going to be more about you than about me.

About you, and for you.

So before we go any further, I want to ask for your active participation. I want you to think back on a moment in your life when you felt totally overwhelmed—a moment when you really wondered how you could ever have gotten yourself into this spot. Right now, try to relive that moment, not just in your thoughts, but also in your heart and in your gut. Can you feel it?

Good. Now just hold that feeling for a moment, while I tell a little story.

Once I had the opportunity to meet a very successful film director at his home in California. His specialty was action-adventure movies, with scenes of the hero and his girlfriend (who's always wearing high heels) holding hands as they run through one explosion after another.

When I arrived at the director's luxurious home, I was surprised to find him watching an old Tweety Bird cartoon.

"You like Tweety Bird?" he asked me.

"The truth? I'd love to see Sylvester eat Tweety one of these days!"

"Me too," the director said. "Don't tell anybody, but I get all my best ideas from cartoons." He gestured toward the cartoon that was playing on his wall-sized TV. "Look. There's Tweety trapped in a dungeon with Sylvester the cat. It took a long time to build up to this scene. Sylvester had a carefully laid series of black-hearted schemes that got Tweety trapped like this. But now look what happens. In the ceiling of the dungeon there just happens to be a window, and through the window you can see a beautiful blue sky with a few fluffy clouds. And what do you know, the bars of that window are just exactly wide enough apart for Tweety to fit through. So Tweety gets away real easy. Which is how it always happens in Tweety Bird cartoons. It takes a long time to set up this seemingly inescapable trap, and then Tweety gets away real easy."

Sufferin' succotash! Are you still holding onto that feeling of total helplessness and impotent rage that came over you at the very worst moment of your life? Now suppose I could show you not just how to get out of those situations, but how to avoid getting into them ever again—what would you say to that?

You'd probably say, "Life is not a Tweety Bird cartoon, and anybody who says it is a Tweety Bird cartoon is nothing but a scum-suckin' pig."

Well, please pass the scum. Because at the most difficult moment of my life, when I was sitting in that courtroom, I began to realize exactly what I would have to do in order to survive this situation. And not just survive it, but use it . . . transform it . . . turn it into that little window up in the roof of the dungeon, with the clouds floating by and just enough space between the bars for me to fit through. Which is exactly what I did.

How did I do it?

How can you do it too?

Over the course of this book you're going to find out exactly what it takes. You're going to find out why literally everything that happens to you is actually happening *for* you. You're going to discover the keys for turning even the most challenging problems into opportunities for positive change.

This book is a very personal collection of strategies,

tactics, and biased opinions. It's my take on how to get the most out of you. You don't have to read these chapters in any particular order, and you don't have to agree with everything I say. But if you give some of these ideas a chance in your own life, I think you'll find yourself making a lot of progress fast. I also think you'll find yourself having a lot of fun.

And along the way, you'll learn something very important. It's what I started to learn at that moment in the courtroom: how to react to things my way, leaning forward on my toes, instead of back on my heels waiting to see how things would affect me. If you keep reading, you'll very quickly find out what I mean.

So let's get started. *Who are you when nobody's looking?*

YOUR DNA YOUR DNA YOUR

DNA YOUR DNA YOUR DNA

YOUR DNA YOUR DNA YOUR

YOUR DNA

YOUR DNA YOUR DNA YOUR

DNA YOUR DNA YOUR DNA

YOUR DNA YOUR DNA YOUR

DNA YOUR DNA YOUR DNA

YOUR DNA YOUR DNA YOUR

DNA YOUR DNA YOUR DNA

YOUR DNA YOUR DNA YOUR

YOUR DNA YOUR DNA YOUR
DNA YOUR DNA YOUR DNA
YOUR DNA YOUR DNA YOUR
DNA YOUR DNA YOUR DNA
YOUR DNA YOUR DNA YOUR
DNA YOUR DNA YOUR DNA
YOUR DNA YOUR DNA YOUR

BY NOW everyone knows about DNA. It's got something to do with O.J., right? Something to do with gloves that don't fit, so you must acquit?

Well, excuse me, Johnny, but if only it were that simple. You see, the genetic makeup of every human being includes billions of information bits. The bits are encoded in molecules of deoxyribonucleic acid, or DNA. These molecules are who you really are, in the most fundamental sense. DNA molecules are threadlike and truly enormous. They are packed into the nuclei of your body's cells like rubber bands inside golf balls, and they're very, very tightly compressed. In fact, if the molecules of DNA were extended in a straight line, they would be more than five feet long.

Blah, blah . . . blah.

Zzzzzzzzz . . .

Okay, wake up! Science class is over. Anyway, that's not the kind of DNA we're going to be talking about in this chapter. This is a whole new kind of DNA. No more deoxyribonucleic acid. We're talking about *Distinct Neuron Archetype* here!

Your Distinct Neuron Archetype is the absolutely unique essence of who you are. It's not only who you are when nobody's looking, it's who you are when even you yourself aren't looking. Even when you're sound asleep, your Distinct Neuron Archetype is still going at it, firing off those electrical impulses in your brain in a way that's different from anyone else's on the planet. When Johnny Cochran says, "If the glove doesn't fit, you must acquit," that's his DNA talking. That's Johnny and nobody else. You know it, I know it and he knows it.

What about you? When you say something, does it have your unique, one-special-person-out-of-six-billion-on-the-planet identity? If not, it may be because you haven't really discovered that identity for yourself yet. But that's okay, we're working on it.

Who You Are Right Now, and
How You Came To Be

Just as some people say "toMAYto" and others say "toMAHto," furious arguments have raged for many years in the scientific community over the relative influence of nature and nurture in human development. There have been shouting matches between white-coated Ph.D.s over this issue. There have been fistfights. There was even a terrible food fight in the cafeteria of the Institute for Advanced Study between proponents of the two points of view, which ended in a tossed salad.

I say, let's stop the insanity! Let's just split it down the middle. Half of you happened because you were born that way, and the other half happened because of what took place afterward. But that was then, this is now! You can adapt. You can enhance yourself. You can evolve. You can kick ass. In fact, I want to add another N to the nature versus nurture controversy. It stands for navigation. You can navigate your way anywhere because the D in DNA does not stand for destiny.

We're not going to ignore nature in the discussion that follows, nor are we going to ignore nurture—in fact, we're going to give them quite a close look. But we're not going to stop there, either. Besides focusing on what got you here, we're going to concentrate on how you can get where you want to go. Besides discussing what made you the way you are, we're going to talk about how you can make yourself into what you want to be.

Pablo Picasso, perhaps the twentieth century's greatest artist and certainly one of its greatest salesmen, is the source of one of my favorite quotes. Picasso said, "If you want to see a genius, watch an uninhibited child."

Maybe it was the fact that Picasso was only 4 feet 11 inches tall that gave him such an appreciation of the child's point of view. In fact, quite a number of Picasso's works, which sold for many thousands of dollars, were based on children's drawings and paintings. However he came up with it, the small man was definitely onto something big when he talked about the genius of children.

Picasso would certainly have agreed with my friend George Prince, founder of Synectics (the company that invented the discipline of brainstorming), developer of Octane and a teacher and student of invention. George also understands the inherent genius that each of us brings into the world. Not long ago he told me something that really made an impression. George said, "It's literally impossible to overestimate a person's unused potential."

Let's think about that for a minute. It doesn't mean that everyone can become an opera singer or an Olympic weightlifter, but it does mean that you have the capacity to develop your own unique abilities beyond any limits anyone sets for you, or that you set for yourself.

Say it again! "It's literally impossible to overestimate a person's unused potential."

Those unique abilities—whether they're a talent for playing the piano or for playing the stock market—were built into you at the moment you were born. They are your nature. They are what makes you different from everyone else—which is actually a wonderful thing, although most people try to deny it every chance they get.

Nurture should function to develop these abilities. But, from early childhood, the supposed nurturing of our uniqueness is really intended to suppress it—to get all the little kids to think the same way and give the same answers and don't rock the boat.

As George Prince explained to me, 98 percent of five-year-olds test in the creative genius range on standardized tests. By age ten, the percentage has dramatically fallen to 32 percent—and it continues to fall until there are only a few Einsteins and Picassos up there, leaving the rest of us wondering what makes them so different from us mere mortals. But, as Picasso himself put it, every human being was a genius at the beginning. It's not what we haven't been able to learn; it's what we already knew but were made to forget.

Not long ago I read a newspaper article about the fierce competition in New York City and Los Angeles for admission to highly selective schools. Not high schools, not middle schools, not even grade schools: This was about cutthroat competition for kindergarten. Four- and five-year-olds are being given "intelligence" tests to see whether they can cut the mustard—and the tests aren't easy in any sense of the word. Here's are some sample questions. Let's see how you do:

1. The color of an apple is: _____

2. The color of grass is: _____

3. The color of a banana is: _____

Did you give "brown" as the answer to all three questions? Or "green"? If you did, you would have been undeniably correct. Even "yellow" could probably be considered an accurate response in all three instances. But unless you answered "red," "green," and "yellow" in the correct order, like a good little boy or girl, you would probably have been marked wrong for each question. Not because there are no brown apples or green bananas, but because you're obviously a wiseass. The message is: *Shape up, but do it at somebody else's kindergarten, willya!*

Let's talk about the brain for a moment. Neurons are the basic building blocks of the brain. Each of those daddies is linked to those around it. They all send out and receive both chemical and electrical signals that control all our activities.

At birth and during early childhood, the brain has many more neurons than in adulthood. Around the age of puberty, the brain undergoes a process called "pruning," in which millions of neurological connections die while others settle into the patterns that will be retained throughout life. One theory holds that those neural pathways that are used most frequently in childhood will survive the pruning most successfully. This suggests that habits set down in childhood have remarkable significance for the potential of the adult. So today your brain and even mine are full of neurons—cells that deliver and receive information by means of neurotransmitters and receptors. You were born with them, and they survived puberty, even if very little else did.

You can think of those teeming brain cells as millions of freeway commuters headed home at the end of a workday. There are billions of on-ramps and off-ramps scattered along the freeway, but those paths are highly susceptible to environmental factors. One ramp might be closed for repairs, and another might be too crowded. But when you encounter a situation like that, do you get out of your car and forget about getting to where you wanted to go? Do you let the air out of your tires and just sit there for the rest of your life? Most unlikely. Instead, you look for another exit and another route to your destination. In other words, you navigate! You adapt! You handle it! And you can do that with anything that life throws at you.

The experiences of childhood wire the circuits of the brain as surely as a programmer at a keyboard initializes a computer. The keys that are typed determine whether the child grows up to be intelligent or dull, fearful or self-assured, articulate or tongue-tied.

But that's only half the story. Understanding that your brain can grow and change is integral to the process of inventing the very best you.

Let's lay out the influences that ultimately determine your Distinct Neuron Archetype:

Nature: where you came from genetically

Nurture: what you've been through experientially

Navigation: where you want to go in life—and where you can go, my good friend

Nature

Before you get there, you must figure out where you came from and why you've selected your particular destination. Failure to do this means confusion will reign. If I go out to a restaurant intending to eat a plate of shrimp, but as soon as I get in my car I forget about that intention and focus on whatever catches my eye, I have only myself to blame for missing out on the shrimp. In the same way, you must know who you are in order to chart a course toward the person you wish to become.

To do this, you need to identify your DNA, the one-in-a-billion way that your neurons are wired—it's your brain's circuitry. DNA is the mental filter that processes your perceptions. When you see, hear, taste, smell and feel something, your DNA determines what you think about it. It's the mechanism that allows you to perceive the world as you do. It's your unique emotional and intellectual template.

Let's face it. You can't do much about your genes. In fact, you can't do anything at all about them. Whether it was a gorgeous, beautifully executed swan dive or a cannonball into the shallow end, your parents took the plunge into the gene pool all on their own. You didn't have any say in the genetic blueprint they created for you. But you have many choices in life, and one of the most important is how you think about your origins—about where you came from, genetically, geographically and culturally.

One of the most important battles in the history of the world was fought in 331 B.C. between a Greek army under the command of King Alexander of Macedon, who liked to be called "The Great," and a much larger Persian army led by King Darius, who, it so happened, also liked to be called "The Great." As this battle shaped up, everyone involved realized that it was going to change the course of history. The Persians, because of their superior numbers, were heavily favored, but the Greeks did have a wild card in Alexander, who had an uncanny ability to create upsets. This, then, was the situation on the night before the great battle of Issus. It was not unlike the Super Bowl game in 1969, in which the Baltimore Colts seemed like a sure thing to beat Joe Namath's New York Jets.

And like Namath, Alexander audaciously predicted victory! Just before dawn, he made a speech to his army in which he declared that they were sure to win, for three all-important reasons:

First, the Greeks as a nation came from a rugged, mountainous countryside in which you had to be tough just to get through the day. The Persians, on the other hand, came from a warm country best suited for producing softies who couldn't even sword fight.

Second, the Greeks as individuals had tough guys for their fathers and grandfathers, but the Persians had been soft and lazy for many generations. They liked to eat grapes, they liked to sleep, they liked to have massages, and they liked to wear perfume. The Greeks had herded sheep in the mountains for many generations, while the Persians were probably scared of sheep.

Third, as Alexander was only too eager to point out, "The Persians have only Darius for their leader, while you are lucky enough to have me." In other words, the Colts were quarterbacked by Earl Morrall, while the Jets had Broadway Joe. No contest. The Greeks won, and so did the Jets.

Why did Alexander, at this crucial moment in history, use the issue of family and heredity to motivate his boys? Because he somehow knew how crucial a sense of where we come from is in determining how far we'll get.

My own parents came from Italy. During World War II they struggled and were forced to scavenge and forage in order to scratch out an existence.

When they arrived in Montreal in the early '50s, the family was still very poor—yet the pride my parents infused in me makes me feel as if I'm descended from the Italian aristocracy. I come from the land of beautiful landscapes, as well as splendid food, art and history. To me, Italy is the heart of the planet, and I feel that it's a great gift to be connected with that country, even though my parents made a conscious decision to leave.

Here are three exercises to help you see your personal heritage in a positive light:

Your Family's Mythology

Though you can't do anything about where your predecessors came from, you can definitely apply a positive spin without in any way altering the facts. For example, do you know where your family originated? How far back can you trace your heritage? Is there any way you can find out more? Once you've gathered sufficient information, try writing out the story as if it were a deeply thrilling legend. If your grandfather moved to California in the late 1950s to open a dry cleaning business, describe the cross-country drive in an Edsel as if it were the most daring journey in the history of the world:

When they got to Bumblebee Mountain outside Phoenix, Grandma refused to ride down the slope in that Edsel. "You can bury me right here," she said, "but that is just too steep. Anyway, I've lived long enough. I'm an old woman."

Gramps thought for a moment, staring off into the distance toward the still unseen golden land of California. The kids just watched in silence, wondering what he was thinking and what he was going to do. Finally he turned around and announced, "All right, we're going back to Cleveland. I love my wife too much to put her through all this."

"Isn't there some other way we can go?" the eldest child asked. "We've come so far, it seems like a shame to go back now."

"Hm. Well, let me look at the map," Gramps said. "I guess we could go all the way back up to Flagstaff."

"Yes, yes!" screamed the kids. "No more Cleveland! California here we come!"

Meanwhile Grandma had fallen asleep in the passenger seat of the Edsel. Though exhausted from the journey, she looked so peaceful, like a marble statue.

It's All in the Eyes

Try to find some old photos of your parents when they were in their twenties or thirties—when they were full of life, dreams and hope, with their whole lives ahead of them. Look closely at their faces in the photos, especially the eyes.

Really look . . .

Then ask yourself: What problems were they facing when the pictures were taken? What hardships
and pressures? What were your parents' Distinct
Neuron Archetypes? How did they understand the
world, and how did this help them to build your
family? What insights have you learned from them
that can help you in your own life? As you look into
their eyes, can you see something of your own eyes?

Hugging Your Family Tree

Another great way to get a glimpse into your genetic roots is to spend some time researching your family tree. Listen to stories your parents or older family members tell about your distant relatives. The experience just might shine some light on why you have mathematical ability or musical talent, or on that bald spot that wasn't there a few years ago. A genealogical study to discover your biological and cultural roots will take a little time, but it's not as hard as you might think. Check www.ancestry.com.

Nurture

From the time you were born until this very moment, you've seen, heard, smelled and experienced life. You streaked in high school, or you won the spelling bee. You sat behind Arnold Manges, who liked to make rubber cement balls, or you ate Pop Tarts each morning for breakfast. Out of all these events, some have had a profound effect on your DNA. Ta da! These are your defining moments.

They come in a variety of shapes and sizes, but they are defining because they're etched into the foundation of your true self. You will always remember these moments. You may speak fondly of some, and of others with great remorse, but your defining moments are always easy to retrieve from the files of your memory.

There's also a special kind of defining moment that isn't accessible to your conscious mind until something happens to trigger it. These memories live in the deep recesses of your mind. They have faded for one reason or another, but then some internal trigger is pulled, and the neurons that store those memories start to fire again.

Other defining moments shaped you over long periods of time. They're not really single events but categories of experiences that were repeated again and again, such as your mom tucking you in bed at night when you were a child. You may not remember specific incidents, but you are affected by their accumulation.

One thing is certain: Everything you've been through has combined to make you who you are, and everything that you go through from now on will create who you're going to be. Remember the movie *Back to the Future*? Marty McFly finds himself transported back in time to his mother and father's first meeting. His arrival on the scene causes an imbalance. If a couple of critical defining moments do not occur, Marty's future will change. If Marty's dad, George McFly, doesn't punch Biff and rescue his wife-to-be, she's not going to be his wife! And if George doesn't plant that magical kiss on Marty's future mom at the Enchantment Under The Sea dance later that night, Marty and his sibs are history, or not even that.

Whoa, that's heavy! So are we saying that at any moment a chance of a lifetime could present itself? Are we saying that more attention ought to go into how we get ourselves through each day? Absolutely. Each and every day—in fact, each and every moment—we have choices, and each choice has a potential upside and a potential downside:

Eat the Twinkie, or go work out . . .

Read a book, or watch *Laverne & Shirley* . . .

Speak the truth, or tell a white lie . . .

Once you understand that you always have choices, your days of being a victim are gone. Once you accept the responsibility for making the best choices, you gain the power to control your destiny.

Find your name!

There have been many influences in my life, a lot of DNA's. Each distinctive in their makeup and each with a unique contribution to me. I have spoken to or met or worked with or loved or thought about or punched, wrestled, been impressed with or sat next to or been fired by or appreciated every person on this list. Here they are . . . but just to have some fun, I jumbled the order of their names. Here's my tribute to you all. This is also who *I* am when nobody's looking:

Shane Marsan Ann Marie Reggie Theus Todd McClamoroch Ann Margaret Ingraham Jane Nocito Sharon Roth Regina Cordova Shawn McCoy Lynn Bruton Barbara Laskey Ed Franczek Collette Brooks Joni Wilson-Allen Francine Werdinger Sharon Stuewig Jeff Donaldson Rich Feitler Eric Miller Patrick Edson Orantes Donascimento Roberta Scimone Ruth Lanier David Leurck Melissa Pankove Roger David Mark Thompson Chris Allen Dawn Van De Keere Tim Bucks Short Carol Papazian Fatima Whitaker Mark Noonan David Gaichas Cheryl Sampson Mike Hartmann Johnny Bench Jonathon Ison Stephanie Cohen Benette Chen Mark Sanderson Jamie "Loud" Schwartz Fritz Russ Klein Phil Kongshaug Frank Farina Michael Hefron Michael Hamilton Robert Ryan Buddy Rich Phillip Stanford Jennings Jeff Hartman Laura Abbadessa Jaime Intile Greg Dennis Rodman Richard Purcell Scott Moon Terry Breadon Scott Waller Valerie Nay Mike Miller Bob Carraher Marc Comisar Tim Olsem Chuck D Carleton Ridenhour Chad Goorhouse Marianne Pontillo Bill Vernick Tom Jonas Mark Powers Boothe Ted Power Elise Tonne Tom Selleck Bob Joanis Bob Ferraro Forrest Fairley Tom Massey Steve Young John Szilagyi Mollie Dierckman Allan Dalton Marie Devlin Erica Spranger Ann Bentzen-Bilkvist Matt Fenton Sam Moore Tessa Warshaw Bev Randolph April Heeren April Gibbs Irene Waldman Pam Zirakian Sara Landesberg Shannon Hardy Cam Bryson Clark Huffstutter Barbara Franco John Franco Nancy Reagan Betty Friedan Allen Bianchi Tom Donovan Michael Lupariello Steve Marsan Tony Clinker Johnny Savidge Barb Larkin Robert Scheley Adriana Pozzani Paul Hillen Whitney Lancaster Ron Schroeder Ingrid Nagy William Posey Joey Parsons Keith Edgett Keith McCluskey Jim Messmer John Tullbane Jan Loomis Janet Hulet Janet Sweeney Dave Howe Clare Robinson Richard Marsan Sarah Tyler Michael Matthew Leah Peter Earley Leah Peters Tony Guard Nacio Sanchez Kurt Wilke Robert Cooley Robert Mitchell Kramer David Cassady Bill Paulin Ron Headings Dale Stephenson Otto Christianson Andrew Gohr Justin Ashcraft Nunzio Olivieri Susan Annunziata Tim Coyle Brad Hanawalt Missy Hawthorne Steve Raterman Joe Deters Henry Heimlich Patty McCormick Kurt Aebi Mark Timbie Norrie Wilson Ralph Blessing Nancy Welling Nancy Gaffney James Packer Jack

Gordon Les O'Nan Keith Robinson Bob Haimes Thomas Hustad
George Prince John Lasage Don Julian Michael Mendelsohn Ellen
Guidera Jim Doyle Laura Maria Mario Bannus Hudson Suzanne
Muntzing Larry Fleming Cindy Rudman Kevin Goulet Gary Kopervas
Mitch Sisskind Gus Valen Rolfes Julie McGill Tom Wilson Connie
Williams Ann Holden Gregg Vincent Wes Michael Macke Dyan Griener
Cris Law Bob Murray Paul Gilmore Susan Bell Kathi Siefert Tom Gooch
Sam Wyche Ray Penno Diane Bartell Nicole Ertas Ligia Rivera Rob
Piotrowski Will Papa Bear Bryant Geoff Rochester Brenda Murphy Steve
Klein Tom Van Paris Susan Haunschild Peter Lloyd Mary Hennig Shellie
Hull Kelly McCluskey Inge Lehmann Joy Browning Mary Kay Laura
Bench Skyrpec Jeff Stamp Randy Villars Bud Herzog Jack Voelker Buz
Buse Tom Brady Anja Voigt Greg Noll Thomas Gearhart Chic
Thompson Jane Mannex Kevin King Brian Wininger Andrew Waits Ray
Hartker Donald Behm Priscilla Petty Madeleine Cohen Bob Scarbrough
Phil Kearns Bill Schermund Mike Poirer Kevin Adler Theresa Herd Chris
Breen Steve Lamonte Jim McLean Gary Glenda Philbin Jesse Wild Bill
Whitney Eric Begehr Amy Ryan Lisa Cohen Doug Hall Terry Bryan
Bundy Tim Zimmerman Jenny Zembrodt Chip Deaver Jeff Brown Deb
Damman Brett Dickson Doug Evans Brendan Mahoney Kim White
Brian Delancey Jackie Dillon Meg Kinney Cathy Schlossberg Mary
Morgan Lynne Thomson Leslie Gillock Robert Goodwin Joe Morgan
Paul Schaffer James Cole Sheryl Roth Rogers Kent Findlay Subhash
Mehta Victor Gielisse John Hawkins Ling Lucas Mari Belczynski Patrick
McNally Charna Linder Cindy Ricciardi Mark Levinson Maria Tomei
David Cwikowski Sayan Ray Mellisa Prusher Gale Sayers Chuck
Maniscalco Arla Gomberg Karen Aktouf Bob Corona Carmine
Melignano Susan Lapointe Sven Risom Tom Crawford Susan Pinter
Chris Gagnon Marcia Moll Ted Woerhle Larry Hughes Paula Comisar
Denise Krienik Chris Almasy Christine Dilandro Theresa Andreoli Dave
Bavis Tonya Blythe Dan Brannen Ray Bozzacco Drew Brinkmeyer
Hubert Irma Beutmueller Wilson Carey Italo Tajo Lori Vehmas Falkin
Dave Germano Chris Gempel Rachel Ellis Vanessa Jackson Bill Crosset
Antoinette Crockrelle Mike Becce Tom Magnus Rebecca Noel Robin
Bruen George Burnett Bill Klump Mark Peiser Ginger Kent Becki Meyer

Ed Vlacich Mary Ellen Vicksta Mark Serrianne Karen Guiterrez Chuck Hong Terry Koritz Sue McNeley Jim O'Connell Pat McCabe Anne Marie Connors Tracey Bender Troy Dennis Buttlewerth Meredith Barone Wendy Ezgur Steve Drucker Nancy Wine Deborah Zimmerman Chris Shimojima Mazen Jawad Alice Petizon Suzanne Mernyk Amy Sullivan Scott Lutz Ezzy Languzzi Nanako Mura Chris Taylor Matt Wilson Janice Waszak Reyna Hlishio Lorenzo Malfatti Inelda Tajo Bruce Chatterley Randy Geller Greta Keifer Brooke Hurt Laurie McSwain Jon Morgan Franco Shirley Antonio B. J. Wayne "Box" Miller Jude Blake Steve Cook Arun Prabhu Sue Wellington Greg Bradshaw Gary Walters Larry Schweer Kim Kathy Hannah Buchanan Harry Rolfes Cliff Weinstein Art Stiefel Dave Truman Art Linkletter Peggy Dyer Alexis Fried Mike Gearin Karen Ridley Cyndee Whitney Mark Michaud Bill Sullivan Montel Williams Wanda Jackson Lori Morro Brian McAuliffe Lynn Carpenter Kimberly Haller J. F. Jomphe Scott Strong Ron Shilliday Jim Cusack Matt Trebon Jim Colafrancesco Benny Hoff Reinhard Sefferitz Lisa Schumacher Kimbra Fox Helen Rockey Kathy Popp Mo Siegel Chip Bergh Mike Bergeron Chris Bean Bobby Cheri Anderson Jane Abrahams John Anost Phil Heimlich Tim Benton Joe Godar Stephen Gillen Mary Frank Gohr Chris Bacon Shirish Mehta Sandie Glass Sherry Brickin Jill Jamieson A. G. Atwater Brian Swette Mary Duffy Spider Cantley Ron Kinnamon Judy Chang Cody Susan Spiegel Kari Matula Jeremy Daniel Nathan Coppock David Germano Dale Crowe Miro Odic Jon Harcharek Gretchen Polhemus Russ Thompson Tracy Tedesco Dave Buck Melody Nobis P.J. Sinopoli Sarah Schultz Shelby Logan Makena Stacy Savidge Don Becker Jim Boerger Robert Saffron Dana Delphia Mike Gorsche Sheila Mardahl Eric Anderson Hank Bias Trish Halamanadaris Michael Audette Sheldon Roesch Dick Joslin Brian Barton Matt Selden Arlene Decker Megan Donahue Mari Power Bill Hogan Tino Mantella Chet Moss Jay Quilty Jennifer Cooksey Barb Korn Nick Podratsky Josephine Dinatale Clare Farber Suzanne Forbes Amy Fovel Sara Frank Mike Felton Brandon Frerking Mary Beth Friesz Larry Rhonda Sheakley Laura Shapira Anna Saurbier Bart McPhail Mark Townsend Deni Tato Alex Olmsted Christina Lin Austin Partridge Warren McCleland Jane Anderson Tracey Addison Dwayne

Howell Randy Mazzolla Margrock Hayes Minor Sona Bhatt Sandra Terry Kirsten Tangeman Ramon Arguedas Nelson Brizuela Nick Capurro Reon Carter Jeri Holschuh Eric Humbert Christine Hanson Fetzer Laura H. Rich Hertlein Danny Hahn Leslie Heckman Noel Heineken Grant Haggard Lori Hogenkamp Ellen Miller Sonet Patty Eddy Deepak Chopra Pam Erickson Lou Ebbling Stacy Stein Liv Blumer John Yerow Glenn Younger Pezzin Khadeja Salley Caprice Corbett Claudia Catania James Conlan Mario Edda Meneghel Chris Joyce Jerome Conlan Mike Johnson Dennis Crawford Michelle Carter Jill Crane Carol Crittendon James Copens Kalena Del Rosario Walter Leaphart Mills Lane Jane Krakowski Robin Jennings Molly Buquo Miki Reilly Howe Joe Resendes Marcie Penno Tommy Beale Liam Killeen Diane Iseman Stan Musial Floyd Patterson Michelle Martin Eric Brody Arden Dufford Jim Ryan David James Brooks Wilson Tom Wilson Arlene Bisulk David Wecker Barb Dilz Casey McLaughlin Lisa Hunt Kathy Gold Linda Schwendeman Ed Stukane Craig Savage Dan Davenport Pam Edelstein Tom Hunter Dave Rinaldi Tessa Westermeyer Gillian Parsons Deb Price Lee Petzelt Michael Katz Phil Gaible Dean Ilijasic Tina McElroy Tamaria Monday Julie Mitter Scott Yanow Mike Bonnie Roe Cam Herrington Chris Ketteman Cara Kirby Mark Gayle Clinker Vicki Mary Joann Lindner Helen Levine Cheryl Law Guerrino Marsan Joe Walter Ted Stephens Annie Biegelson Todd Worrell Jay Silver Wally Dunlap Maureen Murphy Jeff Jacobs Jill Murray Bob Vince Jimmy Rinaldi Mike Neff Karen McCreary Jeanna Lucas Andrea Meneghel Rick Wray Elyse Kane Brian Wells Kathleen Horner Andy Schuon Denise Muennich Vince Gardenia Pat Cooper Howard West Sammy Kahn Tom Denisco Kitty Neal Burton Gilliam Steve Benjamin Andy Beach Dave Goldstein Pat Berry Carl Iseman Dave Spiros Traci Niehaus Mary Ann Naples Muriel Nellis Richard Garrison Dwayne Larson Tom Penders Don Pinkel Mel Stottlemeyer Sheila Pohlkamp Bob Renner Jay Jon Vitsas Jesse Wilde Shirley Delibero Peggy McHale Robert Joseph Joe Molly Sarakites SARK Leo Buscaglia Harry Barrett Tom Feitel Carol Ann Mary Sylvia Peters Mike Lipari Dave Uhlman Josh Burdick Tim Grote Joe Birkenhauer Wendy Wildfeuer Robert Bruce Frankie Stein Johann Cruyff Robert Llewellyn Bill Boggs Rick Harriman Sergio Zyman

Cheryl Perkins Topper Pardoe Marilyn Wilson-Hadid Carol Molina
Donna Neal John Griewe Wendy Kritt Markus Leuker Fritz Grutzner
Lisa McPherson Nancy McPherson Rob Vatter Betsy Westlake Burch
Riber Ed Vlacich Deb Deuling Kristi Bridges Lori Howard Lee
Wiegolinski Denise Spirito Kathy Godocik Antoinette Amorim Janet
Tobias Alecia Swasey Carol Austin Brian Barton Dana Carey Juli Cavnar
Esi Eggleston Mike Gearin Boomer Esiason Linda Goralski Maria Quilty
Dawn Houghton Calvin Stovall Pam Del Rio Lori Collard Bill Daily Dina
Howell Kim "call me" Kasee Donna Summerville Gayle Franger Roger
Frye Laura Brickey Laurie Bryce Meredith Barone Jill Palmer Susan Boe
Fred Keller John DiCola Mark Baltimore Liz Terry Karl Kuhn Mike Roe
Mike Vogt Christy Healy Allison Silver Larry Fleming Chris Sabo Kenny
Parmer Brent Sinclair Leslie Kropp Nikki Angelo Rob Burt Ray Edwards
Amy Wolfe John Ryan Bob Barron Sheila Jackson Teresa Humphreys
Tiffany Wallace Jennifer Petersen Dennis Cheuvront Barbara Laskey
George Clinton Randy Pohl Jim Capo Scott Scharfenberger Amy
Wilson Thomas Glenn Steve Showalter Nancy Harbutte Bernie
Greenberg Stephen Miner Melissa Cunnigham Terry Hamad Jim Merkl
Tim Condron Evander Holyfield Jerry Springer Paul Schaeffer Jim
Knippenberg Carl Yastrzemski Bill Cunningham John Phillips Beth
Snider Julie Benlevi Mary Zoller John Feiler Jeni Dinkel John Kasich Tom
Licata Gregg Smith Sarah Miller Tony Arrasmith Jim Borgman Ariel
Ford Jeff Landis Mary Aarons Alice Kent Barb Moran Ravindra Yande
Robert Laurie Dennis Janson Pat Berry Jeff Ruby Rickelle Ruby Mr.
Scarborough Madeleine Schiro Mr. Yenowine Homer Evans Steve
Woodie Bunny Whitaker Karen Mize Eric Mize Tracy Duckworth Doug
Spak Terry Barnett Barb Heltman Jeana Lucas Terry Gilliam Jo Fuller
Jack Linkletter Kelly Lynch Ernesto Levy Rhonda Nassif Deb Haas Jim
Plecki Kathleen DeLaura Anne Burroughs Amanda Ireland Doug
McCorkle Peter Madigan Stacy Deprey Brian Hutzel John Richards
Mark Mendenhall Stephen Hightower Joe Eley Joe Sain Bill Krueger
Ms K Sugawas Linus Aneke Drew Hibner Chris Mings Michael Sands
Doniel Saddler Greg Stephenson Joe Boxer Gator 8 Steve Malone
Chris McKinney Pam Taylor Denise Anderson Mark Thompson H. T.
Muir Theresa Schorr Julie Barrett *Sorry if I missed anyone . . .*

You may never have met any of the people in my list, but I hope reading all those names will be a useful stimulus for creating your own list. Think of all the people who have helped make you the person you are today. One person's name will pop into your head, and that name will lead to another. Write them all down in the order they occur to you—but be careful, because you'll quickly realize you could spend the rest of your life at this. Thousands of people have passed in and out of your life, and each one has been an influence on who you are and how you look at the world. As you write down these names, what memories come up? What pictures flash across your mental screen? What are the things you regret? What are the things you're proud of? Which names make you feel like picking up the phone and giving those people a call? What kind of effect do you think a call like that would have on the various individuals? What kind of effect would it have on you?

The purpose of this trip down memory lane is to uncover all the people and stories that make up who you are and how you got that way. This is tremendously valuable in its own right, and it's also important for the two exercises that follow.

A DNA Timeline Exercise

We've all lived through events that have left indelible impressions—incidents and episodes that have contributed to defining our essence. Sometimes they're good. sometimes bad, sometimes happy, sometimes sad. But in each case, for some cosmic reason, at the time such an event occurred, you decided to take a mental snapshot of it and store it away for reference.

Now it's time to retrieve that snapshot. This exercise is designed to help you retrieve your defining moments from the recesses of the past. Take a look at my DNA timeline below. See how I completed the exercise, then take a shot at completing your own.

My DNA Timeline

- Born in Windsor, Canada.
- Grew up in an Italian family, oldest of four children
- Moved to Cincinnati
- Trip to the Tetons
- Building a tree fort
- Crush on Pam Enneking in fourth grade
- First time I got drunk (Pabst Blue Ribbon Beer)
- Fell in love with high-school sweetheart
- Won state soccer championship
- Joined the Air Force
- Fell out of love with high-school sweetheart
- Went to college in California
- Returned to Cincinnati
- Got married

- Lost a best friend to leukemia
- Joined the Leukemia Society of America as a volunteer
- Started my first company
- The birth of my son, Shane
- Sold my company
- Organized the World's Largest Chicken Dance (Guinness World Record)
- Got a divorce
- Helped invent Crystal Pepsi and Lipton Originals Iced Tea
- Appeared on *Dateline NBC* and *The Montel Williams Show*
- Had a tumultuous and wonderful love affair
- Started the Sawtooth Invention Company
- Became friends with Gary Kopervas
- Introduced to Mitch Sisskind
- Wrote *Who Are You When Nobody's Looking?*
- Joined Synectics in Cambridge, Massachusetts

Set aside some time to create your own DNA timeline. Start by thinking of some events that jog your memory. It might be an argument with a brother or sister, a first love, a family vacation, the first time you heard the expression "Go for it," or what you were doing at an important moment in history, such as the first moon landing or the first cloning of a sheep.

As you list these moments, look for insights within them. That fight with your sister may have taught you more about forgiveness than anger, and that cloning of a sheep may have taught you something too. Well, it *may* have!

Defining Moments

As you relived the moments of your DNA timeline, what did you turn up? Were you reminded of something you tucked away for years? Does any particular event stand out for its great effect on you?

Take some time to reflect on one of the moments and the way it helped shape who you are. It could be a positive or negative event, or it could include a situation in which you did absolutely nothing and that you wish you could live over again. Here's one of Gary (Creator of *Out on a Limb* comic strip) Kopervas's defining moments:

I always liked to draw as a kid. I remember drawing The Incredible Hulk and Thor when I was five years old. My parents would always drag out my most recent creations, whenever relatives would visit, and bask in the gracious applause of my aunts and uncles. One uncle in particular decided it would be a good idea not to waste this talent on stupid drawings of superheroes and to put it towards a commercial venture—his commercial venture. My uncle asked me if I would draw a picture for an ad he was planning to run in the local paper for his home improvement business. Realizing I didn't know much about the home improvement business, I figured I'd go with what I knew. So I made a picture of The Incredible Hulk installing a storm window. I quickly discovered I couldn't draw storm windows. So, I settled for drawing a man in some kind of uniform sitting on top of a roof.

The ad ran with my drawing! I remember racing home from school so I could open the paper and look at the ad. By the time I had gotten home from school, my mother and father had already bought the paper and left it open to the all-important page. When I saw my work in the newspaper, I remember my body going cold. The rush of excitement left me tingling and light-headed. I remember the looks on my parents' faces as they cut it out and stuck it under a magnet on the refrigerator. The four of us, including my sister, stood there looking at this odd man sitting on the roof of the house as if he were the Mona Lisa and the Hotpoint refrigerator were the Louvre. Once I experienced the exhilaration of seeing my work in print and seeing the reaction of my family, I was hooked. I kept drawing and went on to win several school poster contests.

A defining moment for me was seeing that it was possible to turn India ink and paper into an expression of yourself that other people could look at and enjoy. It left a great impression that still guides me today. In the past ten years I've created thousands of comics that have appeared in newspapers and magazines around the world. I've written material for the comic strips *Out on a Limb, Hagar the Horrible,* and I have a new syndicated comic strip called *Brain Wedgies.* None of this would have happened had I not drawn that grinning guy and that ugly, glowing house.

. . .

Write one of your defining moments in this space or on a separate piece of paper:

_____

_____

_____

_____

_____

_____

_____

_____

_____

_____

_____

_____

_____

_____

_____

_____

_____

_____

_____

_____

_____

_____

Navigation

Navigation is the process of getting from one place to another—physically, emotionally and spiritually. You may have done it without much awareness and foresight, or you may have carefully planned every inch of the journey, but somehow you navigated yourself from your crib to your current place of residence. And there's no going back! So from now on, it will behoove you not just to navigate, but to navigate well.

Good navigation is the key to personal transformation. It's simply a process of understanding your DNA and consciously using it for your chosen purposes. And surprise! Once you start doing that, you'll see that you can change everything, even your Distinct Neuron Archetype itself. Because . . . **DNA is not destiny!**

Please read that sentence a dozen times! I'll wait.

Finished reading? I hope you now understand that your DNA is both the tool for achieving your objectives and the beneficiary of the objectives you achieve. The choices you make and the paths you take should ultimately be guided by the inner voice of your Distinct Neuron Archetype—and if they are, that voice will keep getting clearer and stronger and more deliciously mellifluous (I learned this word recently and wanted to show off—it means "smoothly").

In short, you have the power to shape your

Distinct Neuron Archetype however you please over the course of your life. And it's in this molding and shaping that the true potential for personal growth lies.

Most people, sadly, never take control and actually mold and shape themselves. Instead, they allow their DNA to just be. Like driftwood floating at sea, they let themselves be battered around by the surf for their entire lives. For these unfortunate souls, the fat lady never gets around to singing. In fact, the fat lady has simply left the building once and for all.

But that's not you! The fat lady is still very much present. You really do have the power to navigate yourself to any destination in life. This is the power to forge your own future from whatever past you hold within you. It is, however, a personal choice. No one can will it upon you. If you see the world as a dung heap, nothing, including discovering your true life path, will make it seem worthwhile. Conversely, when you see yourself as a winner, in the zone, kicking ass, getting the love you deserve, achieving success, then you're navigating with power—you're thinking and feeling and living life with zeal and exhilaration because you know you are worth it.

Carlos Castaneda wrote, "So each path is only one of a million paths. If you feel that you must navigate along a route, you need not stay with it under all circumstances. Any path is only a path. There is no affront to yourself or others in leaving it, if that is what your heart tells you to do. But your decision to keep on the path or to leave it must be free of fear and ambition. Look at every path closely and deliberately. Try it as many times as you think necessary.

Then ask yourself one question: Does this path have heart?"

Ultimately, all paths are the same. They all lead to the same place. We're all going to end up in the boneyard. The slab orchard. The worms will crawl in and the worms will crawl out, the worms will play pinochle on your snout. So, when the last man is out, the only question that's really going to matter is, Did my path have heart?

So how can you tell if your path has heart? It's simple—but not always easy: You must ask yourself whether the direction you're going is really congruent with your most fundamental needs, gifts and aspirations.

What do you really want?

What do you really have to offer?

What do you really hope for?

Understanding your needs and your wants is integral to navigating yourself from the person you are to the person you want to be. Setting realistic goals is also fundamentally important, because any creative enterprise is most productive when it includes clear and attainable results. Your DNA—which both causes and is affected by the processes of nature, nurture and navigation—can be a powerful force in your process of self-discovery. Life often can be a self-fulfilling prophecy. If you believe something hard enough, for long enough, it eventually becomes a reality. Shouldn't it be something you consciously decide upon, rather than something that just happens? Your DNA is like a blank canvas. There are no numbers to paint by or lines to stay within. There are just you and a palette and the canvas. What types of masterpiece will be yours—classical, romantic, modernist or impressionistic? Which Distinct Neuron Archetype is uniquely yours? We'll spend the rest of the book helping you find out.

THE NOT-SO-SECRET FORMULA FOR HAPPINESS

THE NOT-SO-SECRET FORMULA FOR

HAPPINESS   THE NOT-SO-SECRET

FORMULA FOR HAPPINESS   THE

NOT-SO-SECRET FORMULA   FOR

HAPPINESS   THE NOT-SO-SECRET

FORMULA   FOR HAPPINESS   THE

NOT-SO-SECRET   FORMULA   FOR

HAPPINESS   THE NOT-SO-SECRET

FORMULA FOR HAPPINESS   THE

NOT-SO-SECRET   FORMULA   FOR

HAPPINESS   THE NOT-SO-SECRET

THE NOT-SO-SECRET FORMULA FOR

HAPPINESS THE NOT-SO-SECRET

FORMULA FOR HAPPINESS THE

NOT-S FOR

HAPP CRET

FORM THE

NOT-S FOR

HAPP CRET

FORMULA FOR HAPPINESS THE

NOT-SO-SECRET FORMULA FOR

HAPPINESS THE NOT-SO-SECRET

IN THE obituary of Roberto Goizueta, the CEO of Coca-Cola, the *New York Times* pointed out that Mr. Goizueta was one of the few people in the world who actually knew the chemical formula for making Coke. The secrecy of that formula is one of the great legends of American business—but why is it such a secret? Even if you knew the formula, you couldn't just open up a bottling plant and start competing with one of the most powerful corporations in the world. Aside from the thousand and one other practical problems, the lawsuits would definitely put you into bankruptcy. So while the secrecy of the Coke formula is a great public relations angle, just knowing the formula isn't really worth much if you can't use it. In contrast, the formula you'll learn in this chapter really is of great practical value—and I'm not even trying to keep it a secret! I strongly urge you to write this formula down, say it out loud, and learn it by heart. Knowing it may not be the key to total fulfillment and happiness, but not knowing the formula can definitely make self-invention much more difficult.

So here it is:

DNA/X = Happiness

A formula for happiness, and I'm giving it away! Best of all, it seems like such a simple formula— nothing like those mean old things on the blackboard in junior high school. This one is really very simple. You already know that DNA is your Distinct

Neuron Archetype. Your true nature. Your dharma. Your karma.

In other words, your DNA is who you really are, and from this you've created a picture of who you really want to be. To use the formula, then, simply divide your DNA by X, and you arrive at your happiness quotient—the sum total of happiness you can expect from your sojourn on earth! But wait! "What is X?" you demand to know, and it's a good question—because the higher this number is, the worse off you will be. You definitely need to find out about X, because that mysterious "X" factor can keep you from getting what you want in life. It can really make a mess of things. So without further ado: X stands for unrealistic expectations! Basically, these come in two varieties:

Good & Bad

Of course, all unrealistic expectations are actually bad. But some people focus on unrealistically positive notions, while others choose negatives. They see only gloom and doom on the horizon, from now until the end of time.

All unrealistic expectations do have several things in common. I believe they all derive from a mindset of victimization and self-pity. There might seem to be a great difference between people who think they're going to win the lottery and people who expect the sky to fall—but the difference is more apparent than real. Both categories of unrealistic expectation set you up for disappointment and bitterness. Both start from an outlook of deprivation and want. The only difference is that so-called positive unrealistic expectations are really strategies for creating disappointment, while the negative version takes the disappointment that's already there and makes sure that it continues indefinitely.

Unrealistic expectations also assume that responsibility for your success will be taken care of by something "out there," rather than by what's "in here." Whether it's the lottery or some other flavor of pie in the sky, it's just a matter of waiting for the big ship to come in, instead of setting sail for yourself. Oscar Wilde said, "Responsibility is what we expect from somebody else." And it's true: most people dread accepting responsibility. That's just a fact of life. We see it happen every day. We find ourselves getting angrier and angrier sitting there in the doctor's office reading old *People* magazines, because the appointment was for ten and now it's twenty after— and we don't stop to think that we forgot to mail the rent or the car payment. We can see ourselves reaching a peak of righteous indignation because a business contact was supposed to call at noon, and now it's almost two o'clock and the phone still refuses to ring, but we don't stop to think about the calls we ourselves have forgotten to return while we've been so busy stewing. We can see ourselves writing an angry letter to an airline because a flight was delayed—but we don't write an angry letter to ourselves when we're late for something, even though that might not be a bad idea at all.

Dear Marc,

The other day I opened the refrigerator and noticed some leftovers that have been there since the final episode of Laugh-In. *For the life of me, I can't understand how this is allowed to take place in a home with running water, electricity, telephone service and all the other trappings of modern civilization. Can't you do something?*

Please!

Best wishes from yourself,
Marc

We can see avoidance of responsibility all the time. And here's something else that turns up just as often—we can see people who aren't as successful as they wish they were, either personally or professionally. Do you know there's a connection between these two very common phenomena? I hope you understand that it's in your best interests to take responsibility for everything you do. But that's only the beginning. I'm also going to suggest that, many times, it's even best to accept responsibility for the mistakes of others. I can hear you saying "What!? Accept responsibility for somebody else's screwups? Why would I want to do something like that?"

• • •

Well, Let's See . . .

In 1974, what looked to most of us like an enormous publicity stunt turned out to be a turning point in the women's movement. A moment in time when responsibility was redefined.

Bobby Riggs, a spry, sassy, pain-in-the-ass, ex-Wimbledon champion believed that men were so superior to women athletically that he, twenty years after his prime, could beat the best female players in the world. He started by challenging the Australian Margaret Court, at that time the top-rated woman player in the world. In a televised match, Riggs essentially destroyed her—not only with his wicked drop shots, but also by manipulating the media so well that Court seemed beaten before the first ball was struck.

The Riggs-Court match was a severe blow to women's tennis and to the whole notion of equality between the sexes. Riggs seemed to be saying that women couldn't really play and that the networks might as well televise sixth-grade softball games if they expected us to watch female athletes. This was too much for Billie Jean King, perhaps the best-known woman player in the world, who more than anyone else had created interest in women's tennis. She challenged Riggs to play her in the Houston Astrodome before a worldwide television audience.

The match soon began to take on a life of its own for Billie Jean, as she started to feel the pressure and expectations of her entire gender. Women (and also a lot of men) across the country wanted Billie Jean to beat Bobby Riggs, not just because Riggs was an obnoxious media-hound, but because she was a genuinely superior player who wouldn't be intimidated.

By the time of the match, the event had become a cross between a Muhammad Ali fight and the first moon landing. The entire world was watching this strange spectacle, in which Billie Jean was carried onto the court by a group of musclemen dressed as Roman slaves. Howard Cosell, the announcer for the match, commented from beneath his toupee that Billie Jean would actually be quite attractive if she would just let her hair grow.

Despite the circus atmosphere, the games themselves were very serious and intensely played. It was certainly a serious matter for Billie Jean King. This wasn't about a woman competing in a man's world. It was about a champion who happened to be a woman—and who accepted the responsibility that greatness imposes. Because of that courage, she reshaped the way the world thinks of athletes.

I've always felt that accepting responsibility is one of the highest forms of human maturity. A willingness to be accountable, to put yourself on the line, is really the defining characteristic of adulthood. Anyone who has raised children knows how true this is. Just look at a baby during the first few years of life. Every gesture, every facial expression, every tentative word has one message for the baby's parents:

"I am totally dependent on you. I can't do anything for myself, and even if I try, I can't be held responsible for the consequences. After all, I'm just a baby!" Ten or twelve years later, of course, as the child enters adolescence, the message to parents will be very different. It will sound something like this: "Why don't you just leave me alone? I want to be totally independent. I don't want to do anything but think about myself. I certainly don't want to accept any responsibility for anything beyond my own very well-defined needs and desires."

It's only when we're at last grown up that these messages—"I am totally dependent on you" and "I am totally independent of you"—finally turn into "You can depend on me," which is the truly adult outlook. Strange as it may seem, of course, there are people in their thirties and forties who are still acting like adolescents. And there are even people in their forties and fifties who are still acting like babies as far as their attitude toward responsibility is concerned. These kinds of people can be hard to have around, especially if you have to work with them, but the large number of people who shirk responsibility can also provide opportunities for you if you are determined to not be like them. If you decide to be one of the few who embrace responsibility, you can lead and you will deserve to lead—even if you never lead anyone but yourself.

Sooner or later, all of us face situations in which we must decide whether to accept responsibility for a problem or to look for ways to avoid responsibility. Assuming that you have in fact done something that has caused a problem of some kind, let's look at the various options and decisions that are now open to you.

First, there's the role played by intention. In other words, was the outcome of your action what you intended it to be—and if it was not, should you still accept responsibility for that outcome? In many areas of the criminal law, the intention to commit a crime must be present in order for the accused to be held criminally responsible. This intention is something quite different from mere negligence. If you leave your garden hose lying across the sidewalk and the mailman trips over it and breaks his leg, you may be held responsible in a civil suit, but you will not be prosecuted as a criminal, as you would be if you had used a weapon in a robbery or an assault.

But we don't have to enter a courtroom to see the important role intention plays in accepting responsibility or assigning it to others. Don't you remember when you were a kid and you left the screen door open so that the cat ran outside and was lost all afternoon? What did you say to avoid responsibility? You said, "I didn't mean to do that." You said, "It was an accident." As I pointed out earlier, there are lots of people who still use these childlike rationalizations well into middle age, but when you decide you want to be an adult, you begin to see that the whole question of intention is nothing more than another opportunity for excuse-making, and you should refuse to participate in it.

The great thing about excuses—and the really dangerous thing about them—is that no matter what happens, excuses are always there waiting to be used. Anybody can have an excuse for absolutely anything, and people have never been better at it than they are today. But the downside of excuses, even good ones, is that nobody really believes them. No matter what people tell you, if you make excuses they're going to know it and they're going to think less of you—but if you refuse to rely on excuses, people are going to know that too, and they'll admire you for it.

This is especially true in business. One of the classic examples happened about fifteen years ago. A widely advertised healthcare product from a leading manufacturer was shown to be unsafe, and the company responded by pulling every single box off the shelves at a cost of millions of dollars. Was the company destroyed? On the contrary! In fact, if they had done anything else, there would have been a tremendous loss of confidence, on the part of both consumers and employees. Instead there was honest acceptance of responsibility for a mistake, and the public image of the company was made stronger than ever.

Contrast this with what happened a couple of years ago to a leading manufacturer of computer chips. When a new microprocessor didn't perform up to expectations, the company made excuses: It was a minor problem, something that would crop up once in a lifetime, and so forth. Were these excuses valid? Maybe, maybe not—but it doesn't really matter, does it? So many people use excuses that nobody really buys them. It's our modern version of the fable about the boy who cried wolf. In this case, the computer chip manufacturer finally took so much heat that they replaced the processors, which is what they should have done in the first place.

So taking responsibility is really the best antidote for unrealistic expectations. If you sit on your porch all day waiting for Ed McMahon to appear with the million dollar check . . . if you drive around behind armored cars waiting for money to fall out . . . if you habitually bet on long shots (or on favorites) . . . if you invest in pork belly futures . . . if you see pie throughout the sky . . . well, then, your expectations are unrealistically positive! You're waiting for the Easter Bunny, or Santa Claus, or Superman. You're waiting for somebody, or maybe for anybody! But this much is for sure: You're expecting something outside yourself and your own DNA to come in and make everything all right!

On the other hand, if you're sure that buttered bread always falls face down . . . if your nickname is Eeyore . . . if you wear a belt and suspenders at the same time . . . if you can't fight city hall . . . if you indulge in these or similar behaviors, then you are definitely a victim of unrealistically negative expectations. And strange as it may seem, you're fundamentally the same as an unrealistically optimistic individual. Both of you are convinced that your future is out of your control.

Almost everyone is affected by unrealistic expectations, unless they become aware of how self-destructive such thoughts can be. As long as you expect things to happen instead of make things happen, you're not going to fulfill the promise of your Distinct Neuron Archetype. Whether you're expecting to win the lottery or expecting the sky to fall is less important than the fact that you're just sitting there expecting and expecting and expecting.

Moving beyond unrealistic expectations is an important part of the self-growth process. It's crucial to begin taking responsibility for your own future (not to mention your past!), instead of looking for explanations and salvation from someplace over yonder.

Recognizing unrealistic expectations means understanding that certain things simply can't be invented! It's unrealistic to invest time, energy and emotion in a perpetual motion machine or in trying to fit a square peg into a round hole. If you're staking your hopes on someone accomplishing that feat, you're dividing your DNA by a very substantial factor of X. By the same token, negative expectations can also be very unrealistic. Buttered bread does not always fall face down, although there are days (even years!) when it seems that way.

Research has shown that the expectation of a positive outcome is always the best predictor of actual success. The real trick, however, is nurturing positive expectations that are tempered by a firm sense of reality—plus a commitment to keep trying, even when the best-laid plans go awry.

So keep this formula firmly in mind:

DNA/X = Happiness

Take it to heart. Memorize it. Use it. Because if you can negotiate the delicate balance between who you really are and what you really can expect from the world, your happiness will always be multiplied rather than divided.

CREATE YOUR HIGH CONCEPT

CREATE YOUR HIGH CONCEPT

CREATE YOUR HIGH CONCEPT

CREATE YOUR HIGH CONCEPT

CREATE YOUR HIGH CONCEPT

CREATE YOUR HIGH CONCEPT

CREATE YOUR HIGH CONCEPT

CREATE YOUR HIGH CONCEPT

CREATE YOUR HIGH CONCEPT

CREATE YOUR HIGH CONCEPT

CREATE YOUR HIGH CONCEPT

CREAT NCEPT

CREAT NCEPT

CREAT NCEPT

CREAT NCEPT

CREAT NCEPT

CREATE YOUR HIGH CONCEPT

CREATE YOUR HIGH CONCEPT

CREATE YOUR HIGH CONCEPT

CREATE YOUR HIGH CONCEPT

IN THE first chapter we discussed your Distinct Neuron Archetype and the three important concepts from which it's derived: nature, nurture and navigation. Now we'll look at another idea that really makes effective navigation possible. It's related to the vision statements or mission statements that many corporations use, but this principle is much more personal and emotional. I call it the *High Concept*.

Imagine traveling by yourself to a place you've never been before, without a map or guidebook. Imagine having to find your way around with only your instincts and the advice of passing strangers. Pretty risky business! Obviously, you'll need a map for the times you get lost, or when you just need to reassure yourself that you're not heading into a swamp.

It's the same with life. We all need an emotional and psychological compass to give us directional signals so that we don't go off the deep end. We need "something" to help us make the best decisions. And what are the best decisions? Simply the choices that are congruent with the bigger picture you see for yourself.

A High Concept is the foundation of your strategy for life. It's your reason for being, and it's what gives your life meaning. It's not an image you create out of the blue. It's an identity you discover for yourself and reveal to everyone around you by the way you behave and the choices you make.

A few examples:

Free your mind and your ass will follow.
                —George Clinton, the father of funk

Everything I needed to know I learned in kindergarten.
                —Robert Fulgrum, author

Drive so fast that you fly over the potholes,
but pull over for family and friends.
                —Bill Posey, Cincinnati lawyer

Fight for truth, justice and the American way.
                —Superman

The two things that people want more than
sex and money are recognition and praise.
  —Mary Kay Ash, founder of Mary Kay Cosmetics

God called me in the morning and asked me
"Would I do good to him, for him alone, and
without reputation?"
                —Florence Nightingale

Have you noticed how complicated life starts to get after the age of eighteen or so? It's like a test, and the questions keep getting harder as you go along. And when you get to the really tough parts, some strange things can start to happen. You can start making excuses, and you can start cutting corners. In terms of navigation, you can start sailing around in circles. Your High Concept is really a kind of sextant that lets you keep your bearings. It answers the question: What do you do better than anyone else?

Before you start going in a direction you can't follow to fulfillment, figure out a direction that fits your
personal strategic competencies.

This process is not the same as developing a company mission statement: We will serve our customers
with the utmost in blah, blah, blah . . . Very mechan-
ical, no emotion, nothing that will really guide
anybody when hard decisions have to be made—
hell, not even when easy ones have to be made. In
contrast, a High Concept is a motivating, guiding
principle that says who you are, with emotion and
thought. This is what you stand for. This is what you
can do well. This is where your true commitment
lies!

My own High Concept, by the way, is:

Purposeful defiance with positive impact

It took me quite a bit of time to arrive at those
five words, but they really express who I want to be
and what I want to do. Actually, one of the most
powerful stimuli for creating my High Concept was
writing this book, and I hope that reading it will
have the same benefit for you. But don't expect to
formulate your High Concept in the short time it
takes to read these chapters. Don't expect to do it in
the next week either, or maybe not even in the next
year. The important thing is to begin the process,
and that is something you really can do right now.
I'll have more to say about the evolution of my High
Concept later in the chapter—and by the end of it,

you'll have made a start toward identifying your own High Concept.

A good way to start is by focusing on specific moments in your life when you really felt you were being the person you wanted to be and also by giving some thought to occasions when you were definitely being someone else!

Everyday Example #1: We've already discussed my experience in family court, listening to the judge lay out the visitation and custody rules for my son and myself. At that moment, I felt like "hulking out," as we used to say. But would that really be defiance? Hardly—because it was exactly what the situation dictated. Probably anyone who's been in that spot has wanted to go through the roof. They're just waiting for you to do that—plus, there certainly would not have been a positive impact, at least not for me. There might have been a positive impact on the judge's kisser, but for me there would have been the slammer. So the real "Purposeful defiance with positive impact" was not just to make the best of the circumstances, but actually to see this as an opportunity to be a much better father than I would have been if it had never happened. Because I would only be able to see my son a certain number of days every week, there would be no excuses that I was too tired to play ball, or too preoccupied with work to talk about school. To turn this obvious time of difficulty into a chance for making things better than ever—

that would definitely be purposeful defiance with positive impact.

Everyday Example #2: Not long ago I saw *Les Miserables* in New York City. It was a great evening, and the performance was especially exciting because I went with my friends Joy and Matt, and Matt's girl-friend Toby was playing the role of Cosette. As the play ended, the whole audience burst into applause —but it seemed to me that this wasn't really enough. I felt that there really should be a standing ovation. But I also felt that I didn't want to be the first guy in the whole theater to get to my feet and stand there clapping. And when I became aware of that hesitation—maybe it was even fear—that's when I knew I was going to do it! Because, more than any-thing else, the "purposeful defiance" in my High Concept refers to defiance of my own negative incli-nations, so I stood up and kept on clapping. Did I shout, "Bravo!" The truth is, I don't really remember. But I hope so.

So what happened? Nothing at first. I was just standing there in the sixth row, and I could feel every eye in the place on me. That's about 5,000 eyes. I felt great—this was definitely purposeful defiance. But what about positive impact? Well, I knew there were basically two kinds of people in the theater at that moment. There were the ones who wanted to give the cast a standing ovation but were too scared to get up, and there were the ones who didn't want to, either because they were deaf or because they were just too grumpy. The more I thought about it, the more I realized I was doing both groups a favor. The scaredy cats were getting permission to act on their true inclinations, and the grumps would at least get some exercise. Within a few minutes everybody in the place was on their feet. It was a great feeling. You see—High Concepts lead you in any situation.

Cognitive Dissonance

This is one of the most important concepts in contemporary psychology—and one of the least understood. Unless you've heard this term before, you probably assume it means thinking about lots of different things at the same time. After all, dissonance in music refers to playing two or more discordant notes at the same time. Cognitive dissonance is somewhat similar, but it really takes the concept quite a bit further.

Cognitive dissonance occurs when your behavior is out of sync with who you really believe yourself to be. This occurs in almost everyone, of course, but as it becomes more pronounced, stress very quickly begins to build. Most of us, for example, like to think we're nice guys and gals. From time to time we all have to do things that aren't nice, and when that happens, a little problem appears on the radar screen. But it's usually easy enough to take care of with some sort of self-explanation or, perhaps, rationalization.

But if the disparity between self-image and self-reality becomes too great, a process of erosion begins to take place in the very soul of that human being! Or maybe even an explosion of some sort. . . .

KA-BOOM! He believed he was very intelligent,
but he kept misspelling potato . . .

KA-BOOM! She thought of herself as a loyal wife,
except when the pool-cleaning man came around...

KA-BOOM! He knew he was a good businessman,
but he had never made any money . . .

A good High Concept is both the best prevention and the best antidote for cognitive dissonance. It should be as short as you can make it. It should be applicable to any situation, neither too business-oriented nor too personal. And it should have enough of an edge so that you don't get bored with it—because when you're bored with your High Concept, you're bored with yourself.

If you're like me, your High Concept will evolve over a long period of time. One day it might just hit you, or you may have to keep whittling away at it. But now is a good time to start.

High Concept Exercises

Finding Synonyms for Yourself

Read through the list of words that follows. The rest of the exercise is a two-step process. First, circle all the words that describe you or that you would like to accurately describe you someday. Then link them together in a sentence that creates an accurate picture of who you are. And remember: Who you really are is not necessarily the person the rest of the world sees at this moment. Rather, it's the person you recognize as your authentic self when the rest of the world isn't even looking. It's who you are when you've looked deep inside yourself and when you've begun to act in harmony with your true inner nature. It's a good feeling!

As you go through this exercise, keep these points in mind:

- Try to link words that don't naturally seem to flow as a unit.

- Free associate. Use your stream of consciousness.

- Don't immediately dismiss a combination of words if they don't instantly click. A well-timed *non sequitur* can often reveal great truths.

- Use more than two words.

- You don't have to only use the words provided. Use a thesaurus or a dictionary if a word from this list doesn't work in your sentence.

Bogus • Charming • Delightful Spectacular • Savory • Spirited Citizen • Vivid • Cheerful Cordial • Alluring • Sexy Genius • Lyrical • Huggable Outdoors • Faithful • Honor Diligent • Olympian • Boundless • Logical • Diverse • Spicy Thoughtful • Peaches • Prestige Real • Childlike Elegant Majestic • Superior • Fun Classic • Entertaining • Worldly Passion • Swift • Roasted Muscle • Hot á la Français • Intellect • Crisp • Gargantuan • Enthralling • Daddy • Fresh • Ripe Rotten • Modern • Breeze • Sassy • Whimsical • Just for Kicks • Giggle Chuckle • Sunny • Riot • Hedonistic • Mischief • Free-Spirited Truthful • Provocative • Compromise • Reputable • Controversial • Point Blank • Uncompromising Rocker • Basic • Heart • Reliable • Open-Minded Constructed • Handmade • Old-World Sophisticated • Bold • Engineered • High-Performance • Uncharted Custom-Crafted • Revolutionary Strong • World-Class • Wizard • Radical Potent • Enriched • Renaissance • Traditional • Mentor • Student Relaxed • Contemporary • Impression Natural • Factory-Sealed • Cowboy • Honest Primitive • Cave Dweller • Wild • Explorer Untamed • Climber • Tropical • Ecstasy • Harmony • Different • Aggressive • Confident • Expert • Secure • Combative • Motivated Practical • Charming • Organized Productive • Argumentative • Capable Well-Bred • Dignified • Poised • Feminine • Vanity • Svelte Robust • Healthy • Energetic Gracious • Poetic • Artist • Articulate • Bright • Astute Vivacious • Kind • Steely • Beefy • Riveted • Sinew Turbo-Powered • Shocking • Ditzy Innovative • Creative •

Off-the-Wall • Feisty • Grounded • Solid Insightful • Motherly • Committed Benevolent • Magnanimous • Reflective Steaming • Modest • Devoted Genuine • Full-Throttle • Dangerous • Rebellious • Magical • Unique Unconventional • Peachy • Guaranteed • Conscientious Baffling • Simple • Ironclad • Vulgar • Essence • Blue-Collar Excessive • Total • Tool • Proactive Resilience • Take-No-Prisoners • Warrior Devout • Do or Die • Compassion • Saucy • Extreme • Clandestine • Wanderer • Purposeful • Conviction Playful

Suppose Abraham Lincoln were doing this exercise. What words would Honest Abe pick? Well, maybe he would select . . . honest! Probably not rebellious, since rebellion was what the Civil War was about. Abe was definitely unique, capable, and articulate, as he proved in the Gettysburg Address. Can you form a sentence including honest, unique, capable, and articulate? If so, you're pretty articulate yourself.

Just for practice try this with a few other well-known personalities. For example:

Phyllis Diller _____

_____

_____

Bugs Bunny _____

_____

_____

Joan of Arc   _____

_____

_____

Jimmy Stewart   _____

_____

_____

When you choose your own words, you don't
have to pick four or five. You may want to begin with
using just two and then see where they lead you. For
example, if you pick the words passion and diligent,
you might then create a sentence or phrase like
"Passionate Diligence" or "Passionate in Work and
Play." Keep your mind open to the possibilities.

A High Concept doesn't have to be two or three
or four words. It can be fifty, provided that those fifty
awesome, incredible words get you to your reason for
being alive and help you understand your distinctiveness!

For attractive lips, speak words of kindness.

For lovely eyes, seek out the good in people.

For a slim figure, share your food with the hungry.

For beautiful hair, let a child run his fingers
through it once a day.

For poise, walk with the knowledge you'll never
walk alone . . .

People, even more than things, have to be restored,

*renewed, revived, reclaimed and redeemed,
redeemed, redeemed.*

Never throw out anybody.

*Remember, if you ever need a helping hand, you'll
find one at the end of your arm.*

*As you grow older you will discover that
you have two hands—one for helping yourself,
the other for helping others.*

—attributed to Sam Levenson

Whatever words you choose, they should inspire action. Your High Concept should read like a bugle call, not like a car leasing agreement.

Possible High Concepts for You!

1. _____

_____

2. _____

_____

3. _____

_____

4. _____

_____

5. _____

_____

Become a Michelangelo of Word Pictures

Metaphors are word pictures that can be extremely useful for describing people. For example:

- She had a smile like the Mona Lisa.

- He was built like a dumpster.

- She had a smile like a dumpster.

- He was built like the Mona Lisa.

Try mixing and matching the metaphors below in ways that describe yourself. See what you can come up with, and write your responses in the spaces below.

A tidal wave	*A lion's roar*
Like a charging rhino	*An arctic blast*
Built like a brick house	*Thinks like Einstein*
Hard-chargin', like Tiger Woods	*Irish Enya Morning*
Deep as the ocean	*A revving engine*
Trains like an Olympian	*Bolt of lightning*
Third-world-like	*Like a classic opera*
A distant train's whistle	*Woolly as a bear*
Like a skipping stone on the ocean	*Italian opera*
A star illuminating the night	*Bad to the bone*

Madonna	*Swift as the wind*
Sultry, strength, sinew	*Strong as an ox*
A cheery songstress	*Freedom is nonnegotiable*
Thundering herd	*Like a lullaby to a baby*
Like a church choir	*Like the sun's brilliance*
Brains, brawn, bawdy	*Right gives might*
Romance novelist	*Treacherous as Everest*
Formula One champion	*Like a jagged rock*
Jimmy Stewart	*Mind like a steel trap*
Braveheart	*Joan of Arc*
Like a mother's kiss	*The Rolls Royce of . . .*
Pail and a bucket	*Butterfly*
A treasure chest	*Cockroach*
Swiss army knife	*Ticker-tape parade*
Like a spring breeze	*Broken glass*
Bacon sizzling	*A feather*
A Yugo	*Jiggly Jello*
A jousting sword	*Athlete's foot*
Fired-up	*Tooth and nail*
Like crazy	*White-hot*
Bit-o'-honey	*Bee's knees*
Whirling dervish	*Waterbug*

Your High Concept (Michelangelo Style)

1. _____
   _____
   _____

2. _____
   _____
   _____

3. _____
   _____
   _____

4. _____
   _____
   _____

5. _____
   _____
   _____

Be Your Own Brand Manager

Think of yourself as a product—a product that has some of the qualities you possess. It doesn't really matter what kind of product. Just think of the aisles of your supermarket and pick a product you like or that you're familiar with. Maybe you're a jar of pickles. Or maybe you're a medium-bristle toothbrush.

Notice how each product has certain qualities that pop out at you? It whitens, it brightens, it smells lemony fresh. Each of these has what is called a unique selling proposition or a reason for being. Each has a clearly spelled-out essence.

"Brand management" is the term used to describe the growth and development of a particular product. The person responsible for the success of a brand is called the brand manager. You can use the same tools that are used in brand management for what we're calling "life management."

Many of the same principles that go into successful brand management apply to life management. For instance, brand management includes the concept of an "equity model," which clearly defines what the brand stands for in our minds and what we can expect it to stand for in the minds of the consumer. Everything we subsequently do for the brand—its ingredients, packaging, promotion and advertising—flows from the equity model. Whether it's hand soap or toothpaste or dish detergent, it needs to have an equity model to succeed in the long term.

Clarifying what a product will never be is also very important. You can't be all things to all people. As important as it is to define who you are, you also have to take time to figure out who you aren't and who you could never be in a million years.

Below, make a list of the traits and descriptors that should and should never be attributed to you:

ME	NOT ME

Write an Ad for Yourself

Think of yourself as a consumer product and write a magazine ad that sells your unique qualities to the potential buyer. Before you start working on your ad, consider these questions:

- What product should I be?

- What are my ingredients? Be creative!

- What does my packaging look like?

- How would I promote myself?

- What would I want prospective consumers to know about me?

- What stores and what part of the store would I be displayed in?

When you know that an advertisement has to get the point across in 30 seconds or less, it can lead to very concise and hard-hitting writing. Here's how Gary Kopervas might describe himself through the metaphor of an ad for an off-road vehicle.

The Gary Kopervas Road Grabber Ad

- *A different kind of Sports Utility Vehicle*

- *Stable wheelbase but still loves to grab the road*

- *Handles well on main streets but prefers to be off the beaten path*

- *Plenty of room for the family*

- *Low maintenance but needs daily refueling (runs on sweat and daydreams)*

- *Cool Bug Guard Grill (optional)*

- *Spare tire discreetly hidden away*

- *Motor idles quietly but never completely shuts off*

The Gary Kopervas Road Grabber

Enjoy the adventure, because there's more than one way to get where you want to go!

If you need ideas to get you going, thumb through magazines on the newsstand and read the ads. Use the *Me/Not Me* list. Remember, you can't be all things to all people, but you need to be completely, absolutely honest. (Okay, so it's not exactly like real advertising!)

Are You a One-in-Five-Billion Man or Woman?

Candice Carpenter has been president of both Q2, Barry Diller's cable network, and Time-Life Video and Television. She was also one of the first women to climb Half Dome in Yosemite National Park. This is how she describes the importance of creating a High Concept for yourself:

"Success is about creating something of personal value, and every person alive defines value in their own unique way. And it doesn't matter whether you're financing a new company, launching a brand online, raising a daughter or scaling a mountain—the process of creating your value requires specific steps. First, imagine what you want to see in the world—something that doesn't exist. Then take a blank sheet of paper and design your dream. Instead of being intimidating, a blank page becomes an open invitation for you to explore, expand and aspire. Second, inspire people around you to become comfortable with the concept of filling a blank page; do this by example and experiment. Third, stick with it through the hard times. If you are committed and if you aren't afraid of the hard times, obstacles become utterly unimportant. The world respects creation. People will get out of your way."

Over six billion people walk the planet. What makes you distinctive? It's not a tattoo or goatee or getting your nipples pierced. You get your distinctiveness from within. Your desires, your dreams, your life, boiled down to a simple set of words. That's your High Concept.

Your High Concept tells you exactly who you are when no one is looking. When your kid does something that puts you over the edge, take a breath . . .

and go to your High Concept. When a friend offers you a cigarette when you just quit cold-turkey the week before, go to your High Concept. You'll find that when you hold yourself to a level of scrutiny and self-analysis, what the world thinks becomes less important. Make no mistake. You are your own judge and jury.

If you've gone through the exercises in this chapter, you've practiced a number of ways to look at yourself. But it's not enough to do the exercises and then stash the results in your drawer and pull them out when you're in a crisis. Now's the time to commit yourself to living your newly discovered High Concept every day. Internalize it. Live it every day. Make it a reflex!

Your Distinct Neuron Archetype helps you understand where you came from and why you think the way you do. Okay, where *do* you want to go? Your High Concept is your map!

DO YOU KNOW WHAT YOU DON'T
KNOW? DO YOU KNOW WHAT
YOU DON'T KNOW? DO YOU
KNOW WHA **DO YOU** W?
DO YOU KN **KNOW** DON'T
KNOW? DO YOU KNOW WHAT
YOU DON'T KNOW? DO YOU
KNOW WHAT YOU DON'T KNOW?
DO YOU KNOW WHAT YOU DON'T
KNOW? DO YOU KNOW WHAT
YOU DON'T KNOW? DO YOU

DO YOU KNOW WHAT YOU DON'T
KNOW? DO YOU KNOW WHAT
YOU DON'T KNOW? DO YOU
KNOW WHAT YOU DON'T KNOW?

WHAT YOU DON'T KNOW?

KNOW WHAT YOU DON'T KNOW?

DO YOU KNOW WHAT YOU DON'T
KNOW? DO YOU KNOW WHAT
YOU DON'T KNOW? DO YOU

YOU KNOW what you're good at, and you know what you're not so good at, right? But what are the things that you're so good at that you don't even know it, things you do intuitively, reflexively, utterly without self-consciousness? Conversely, there are probably areas where you're such a klutz that you aren't even aware of it. I won't ask you what those things might be, because you wouldn't know.

What we're really talking about here is competence and incompetence. Behavioral scientists have identified four different levels of those two characteristics:

1. **Stuff you're really bad at, but you don't know it.** You're terrible at something and you're totally blind to that fact. You're so terrible that even your best friends won't tell you. You don't know how to tie your shoes so that they stay tied. You need five tries to get your car into a parking space, and you assume it's that way for everybody. In short, these are the areas of life in which you haven't yet gotten to square one. You're at square zero. Or maybe square minus one. Peter Sellers's portrayals of Inspector Clouseau in the Pink Panther movies were a perfect example of unconscious incompetence. The inspector thinks he knows all and sees all when in fact he knows nothing and sees nothing. It's a pity he never made a movie with Mr. Magoo.

2. **_Stuff you're bad at, but at least you're aware of it._** This is progress, sort of. You're still terrible, but at least you're aware of it. These are areas in which you can make an effort to improve, or at least make an effort to stay away from. If you were on an airliner, and the flight attendant asked if you'd like to come into the cockpit to see if you could land the plane, you'd probably beg off—possibly because you were too absorbed by the in-flight movie, but more likely because you knew you'd probably land the plane backwards or upside down. Conscious incompetence can be a drag, but in certain situations it can also be your best friend, which is good because this is the mode most of us are in most of the time.

3. **_Stuff you're pretty good at, and you know you're pretty good._** Now you're talking! These are things you do well, you know you do them well, and you make the necessary effort to do them well. Many people are consciously competent in their work. Your job may not be your idea of a good time, but you've learned to take satisfaction in it. When you do it well, you know it and others know it. Even if your job is raising earthworms, at the end of the day you know you've given it all you've got, and you know your worms are as good as the next guy's, if not better. That's conscious competence.

4. Stuff you're so great at that you don't even realize it. This is the highest form of skilled behavior. It's skill beyond skill. You're so good that you don't even think about it! So good you don't even know it! Did you ever hear the Chuck Berry song "Johnny B. Goode"? There's a line that goes, "He could play a guitar just like ringing a bell . . . " What's being described there is unconscious competence. It's doing something difficult as if it were easy—because, for you, it *is* easy. When Willie Mays caught fly balls in center field, he used a kind of basket catch with his glove waist-high. It looked as if he wasn't even aware of making the catch, as though his thoughts were a thousand miles away. And maybe they were.

Right now, let's make up some lists that identify your level of competence in various areas of your life. Our goal will be to move your competence up a notch, or maybe a couple of notches, by introducing a higher level of awareness.

Your first list will probably be rather short. By definition, your areas of unconscious incompetence are invisible to you. But maybe if you think about it, you'll be able to come up with a few things. Give it some thought: Is there anything that you think you do well enough but the results just never seem to bear this out? Hm? Well maybe, as the saying goes, the difference between "champ" and "chump" is "u" . . .

Your areas of unconscious incompetence are:

1. _____
2. _____
3. _____
4. _____
5. _____

Now focus on the things you know you're bad at. You're a failure! You just can't cut it! You're a pathetic excuse for a human being!

Your areas of conscious incompetence are:

1. _____
2. _____
3. _____
4. _____
5. _____

Now let's move on to the positive side of the ledger. Where are you consciously competent? What are the things that you do extremely well, provided you make the necessary effort?

Your areas of conscious competence are:

1. _____
2. _____
3. _____
4. _____
5. _____

Finally, there are probably some things you do so well that you never even give it a thought. Well, here's your chance to think about those things. What can you do as easily as falling off a log—besides actually falling off a log?

Your areas of unconscious competence are:

1. _____

2. _____

3. _____

4. _____

5. _____

If you had difficulty filling in the last section, that's perfectly understandable. After all, how can you identify the things you're so good that you don't even know you're good at them? Believe me, they're there, but you may need some help in finding them. So here's a suggestion: Ask somebody! Find somebody who knows you really well, take that person aside, and in a low voice ask, "Have you ever noticed anything I do really well?" Chances are, there are things like that—because if you think of other people that you see every day, it's almost certain that you've noticed talents and abilities they're not even aware of. Whether it's throwing a football or boiling an egg, we all have areas of unconscious competence—but by their very definition, we're not aware of them until we ask.

Okay—now you have a better idea of who you are, what you're good and not-so-good at, and how distinctive you are from everyone else on the planet. The second half of the book is built to present individualized tactics that will enhance your potential, improve your capabilities, and give you the power, strength and perseverance to invent, inspire and lead the life you really want. Try to make the following tactics a REFLEX, just like the mallet hitting your knee. Use the following tactics, and you'll most assuredly create the life you want. Some of the following tactics may work better for you than others.

So take a big breath, focus on your High Concept possibilities, and jump into the second half of the book! Feel free to refer back to the first half of the book in order to stay on strategy!

THINK NAKED!   THINK NAKED!

THINK NAKED!   THINK NAKED!

THINK NAKED!   THINK NAKED!

THINK NAKED!   THINK NAKED!

THINK NAKED!   THINK NAKED!

THINK NAKED!   THINK NAKED!

NAKED!

NAKED!

NAKED!

NAKED!

THINK NAKED!   THINK NAKED!

GEORGE PRINCE is one of America's most insightful thinkers on creativity and inventive thinking. He has done some pioneering work on realizing human potential. Prince describes how the process of becoming a fully realized personality begins in infancy. Our first and most important guides, trainers and conditioners are our parents, our siblings and our own individual programming. The influence of genetic makeup and instincts also forms an enormously important part of the mix.

From the beginning, the way we interpret events and make them useful depends upon how our own thought processes are organized. Our self-organization determines how we react, interact and accommodate ourselves in any situation. But our primary motive is always to grow, to understand the meaning of the world, and to be more meaningful ourselves. In fact, George Prince says that the desire to be meaningful is the most fundamental need of every human being.

Prince emphasizes that information pertaining to our survival overrides every other kind of stimulus from the environment. And there is one kind of survival information that has a stronger impact than all others. This is the experience of anxiety, which can begin as early as the first year of life. If a mother is anxious during breast-feeding, for example, her anxiety may be communicated to her child. Or if a child is separated from his or her mother, there may be extreme anxiety simply because the capacity to understand temporary situations has not developed yet.

George Prince says that in order to understand the world and its potential threats and benefits, the brain has developed a kind of scanning system that is called the *amygdala*. The amygdala asks every incoming signal two questions: Does this promise to be a nurturing experience? Or is this a possible threat?

If a threat is perceived, the amygdala reacts instantaneously, like a neural tripwire, telegraphing crisis signals to all parts of the brain. If the threat is physical, the amygdala signals fear. But if the threat is emotional, the signal is anxiety. And as we start to grow, thousands of anxiety signals are stimulated by the constant criticism we receive from the authority figures who are all around us at every moment.

> "We all started creatively free . . . remember the sandbox, all we needed was a bucket and a good shovel. Then we went to school, we learned that the chairs were to be in rows and that tree trunks were to be colored brown, if you lived in a world of purple tree trunks, you probably learned to hide it."
>
> —SARK, author of *Creative Companion*

With each criticism, our amygdala signals a very unpleasant circumstance—one that we try to avoid in the future. Gradually we begin to form the idea that the best possible person is one who makes the least number of mistakes. We start to divorce ourselves from who we are when nobody's looking, because we've internalized the idea that somebody is always looking and finding fault. That's why one of the most important and empowering things in life is recapturing the state of mind that existed before the fear of failure set in. It's a matter of telling that little person to come out of hiding, because that little person is an absolute genius, as the graph below demonstrates.

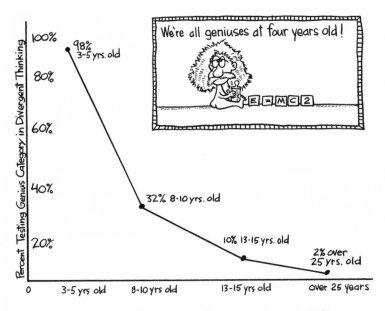

Results of 1,600 children given eight tests of divergent thinking ability show:

Ages 3-5 years, 98% scored in the creative genius category.

Five years later, 32% scored in the creative genius category.

Ten years later, 10% scored in the creative genius category.

In tests of over 200,000 adults over 25, only 2% tested in the creative genius category.

—from *Breakpoint and Beyond* by George Land and Beth Jarman

I like to refer to kids' special kind of genius as *thinking naked.* Here's why.

Kids love the bathtub. It's an environment in which the imagination can roam free. It's an opportunity to be creative, messy and noisy. It's even a chance to get clean.

But getting out of the bathtub is even better. Can you remember what that was like? Out of the tub you ran, tossing the ducky to the right, the towel slithering off your little buns. You were buck naked, laughing the whole time. Life doesn't get better than this. You've busted out of maximum security, you've gone over the top, you're completely uninhibited. You're running—and you're thinking naked too!

Unfortunately, life can't be like that all the time. Sooner or later, we've got to get back into our clothes and get our diplomas and our jobs and our mortgages. But if you can just regain something of what it was like to "think naked" all those years ago, you'll find that some amazing things start happening. And it's also true that if you don't get back in touch with that wild-child exuberance and sense of wonder, you're going to start wondering whether it's worth getting out of bed in the morning.

Laughter . . .

Kids really know how to laugh, and they like to do it a lot. Did you ever notice that five-year-olds laugh much more often than twelve-year-olds—and that twelve-year-olds laugh a lot more than forty-year-olds? Life isn't quite as funny when the rules and regulations start to kick in—and once the rules are internalized, once we've really built them into our hearts and souls, things become very serious indeed. The ability to laugh like a child is fundamental to the ability to see the world as a child—which, by the way, has been the secret of success for some of the most creative individuals of the twentieth century, from Picasso to Disney to Spielberg.

It's also worth noting that some of the most destructive people in history have been notable for their lack of humor. The Communist and Fascist dictators of Europe were good at projecting anger, and they were good at creating fear—but humor? No.

Powerful people and the symbols of power that they like to accumulate are rarely humorous, at least intentionally. Think of those old Russian generals with all those rows of ribbons on their uniforms. Whatever else you might want to say about them, it was obvious that those uniforms were supposed to be very serious. A dozen rows of ribbons, a big red star on the hat, all sorts of gold braid hanging everywhere—hey, this is no laughing matter!

What irony, then, that humor played an important part in the downfall of the Soviet Union. In the final years of the communist regime, political jokes became a highly developed art form in Russia and in all the countries of Eastern Europe—and the generals didn't get the joke until it was too late.

Laughter actually comes in several categories, and it's important to understand the similarities and differences. Have you ever gone to a comedy movie and noticed that the audience starts laughing even before anything funny happens? A leading comic actor can simply come on the screen and make a bland remark about the weather, and everyone in the audience will start laughing. I've seen this happen many times with actors like Robin Williams and Rosie O'Donnell. This used to really puzzle me, until I realized that what lay behind it was a desire on the part of people to have a shared experience. They want to participate in the laughter together. I call this the laughter of community.

Another kind of laughter that can be observed at the movies is something I call laughter of recognition. This occurs when people want to show that they get the joke, that they see how something was intended to be funny even if less-informed or less-sophisticated people don't see it. This kind of laughter is especially common among younger audiences, and I find myself frequently missing out on it. Irony is the basis for so much humor today, and by its very nature irony is intended to exclude a certain percentage of people. The rest of them laugh to show they've been admitted to the club. They laugh to show that they recognize the joke and to be recognized as members of that select group. That's why I call it laughter of recognition.

Polite laughter is yet another category. This is the

sort of sociable nonlaughter that one gets when a laughing response is called for but isn't really motivated. We've all had the experience of telling a joke that doesn't really go over too well and that elicits only polite laughter. And we've all responded to such jokes with polite laughter of our own. It's just a gesture that keeps the ball rolling, but it's an important one. Nobody likes to be on the receiving end of polite laughter, but it's better than being poked in the eye with a sharp stick, to quote an old joke.

The last and most important category of laughter I'll mention might be called real laughter. It's spontaneous. It's happy. It's unpremeditated. It has no hidden agenda. It happens when you see or hear something that's really funny. The more real laughter you can bring into your life, the better off you'll be.

Kids are really our best source of knowledge about real laughter. Look at the way children laugh from infancy through four or five years of age. They really put their whole selves into it. We lose that to a large extent as we get older, and unlike some people in the self-development field, I'm not sure that loss can be completely avoided.

A friend of mine has a little daughter, and I've watched her grow through the first ten years of her life. I was there the day they brought her home from the hospital, and I've attended all her birthday parties. For her third birthday, I bought her a set of colored pencils and a big pad of drawing paper. I was glad to see that these quickly became some of her favorite things. Her parents used to bring me some of the big circles and spirals she drew in all different colors—some of them were really quite beautiful, and there was even a kind of balance to them. I used to hang them up in my house and when she came to visit she'd see them and be so proud.

Then, when she was about five or six years old, her drawings changed. She started drawing stick figures and houses. Usually there'd be a stick figure standing beside a house, which was drawn by putting a triangle on top of a square. The little girl was still just as proud of her drawings, and she saw them as a big advance over the ones she'd done when she was a baby—and they were more advanced in some ways. But they were also less free. There was a sense of responsibility about them, an effort to put everything in the right place and make everything the right color and the right size. I actually had liked her earlier drawings better, and one day I asked her if she could do another one for me in the old style. Of course, she looked at me as if I'd lost my mind. She was very insulted, and as I thought about it, I realized she had a right to be. I was asking her not to grow up. That's like asking a poverty-stricken individual if they're sure they really want to be rich, because money doesn't bring happiness, right? In any case, around the same time my little friend's drawings changed, her laughter changed too. She was no longer thinking naked. She was starting to think fully clothed.

Kids have a lot of concerns and worries that seem as big to them as ours do to us, but they really don't have a lot of responsibilities—they really don't have bills that must be paid by tomorrow, or presentations to make, or phone calls that can make your palms sweat. It's those kinds of responsibilities that suppress real laughter as we get older, and there's simply no avoiding it. But we should try to bring real laughter into our lives as much as we possibly can. It's good for the soul, and there's even been evidence recently that heartfelt laughter has the ability to benefit physical health.

Crying

Just as kids laugh more easily, they also cry more easily. Tears can mean many things. People cry when they're sad, but they also cry when they're happy. The one thing that seems certain about crying, though, is that it's a sign of authenticity. Crying, like laughing, is a profound form of self-expression. It's direct, it's unfiltered and it's from the heart. The mask is off when you cry. The makeup is a mess. That's why crying can be such an important part of thinking naked. This doesn't mean you have to use up a box of tissues every day, but an occasional good cry can definitely get you past the white picket fences of your inner self and into the zone where things really matter. Seeing another person cry can also make a powerful impression, especially when it's someone you look up to.

I saw my dad cry twice in my life—the same guy who had been a refugee during World War II—who had cried himself to sleep each night as a thirteen-year-old because he had to be away from his parents for more than two years. Well, I saw him cry twice

Once was when his father, my nonno, died unexpectedly in a tragic automobile crash, a loss we all felt very profoundly. Nonno was taken much too soon in his life. The sorrow was enormous. The other time also came unexpectedly, a time when my father—the stiff upper lip poster child—was comfortable with showing his emotion.

In 1994, I was lucky enough to take my father to the Italy-Brazil World Cup Final in Los Angeles. The excitement was thick in the air. Balloons streamed skyward, streamers flying, marimba bands played, and to my surprise my always frugal dad ran over to an official World Cup memorabilia stand and bought a really dorky official World Cup hat. We went to our seats near the 40-yard line and joined in the excitement and cheering. The teams were led on to the field and took their place facing the crowd for their respective national anthems.

As the Brazilian anthem came to an end and the Italian anthem began, I felt the emotion stir in my father next to me. My dad, the epitome of decorum, was truly inspired. I strained to look over at him to my left, but I didn't want him to know it. My father, in one of his finest moments, was listening to the anthem of his homeland, watching his team, the "Azzurri" from Italy, with his oldest son.

I could just barely get a glimpse of a tear streaming down his cheek, a tear that I'll always remember. My Dad was happy, and he was crying at the same time. He was once again feeling the world from a child's point of view. In other words, he was thinking naked!

Comedy vs. Tragedy

Modern physics has demonstrated that light can be both a particle and a wave. If we design an experiment based on the assumption that light behaves like a wave, we will find that it does indeed behave like a wave. If we design another experiment in which light is supposed to behave like a particle, sure enough it behaves like a particle. So what really is the true nature of light? There's no simple answer to that question. It's all a matter of perception and expectation.

In the same way, life can be either a comedy or a tragedy, and it is always in your power to determine how you want to see it. I prefer to see it as a comedy, and I highly recommend this to you also. But let me explain exactly what I mean by that. I don't mean to suggest that life is like a comedy you see on television at eight o'clock on Channel 5. I'm using comedy according to an ancient definition of the word—as a progression from sadness to happiness, from a low point to a high point, from poverty to wealth in every sense. In literature, the best example of comedy in this sense is Dante's *Divine Comedy.* Although I don't believe there is a single joke in that entire work, it is a comedy in the sense that the story begins in hell and ends in paradise. Yet most people don't even know that Dante wrote two more volumes that take place after the completion of the *Inferno.* History has chosen to focus on the frightening, painful part of Dante's poem, and if you're not careful you may find yourself doing the same thing in your own life. We live in a time that has equated seriousness with intelligence, unhappiness with sensitivity, and victimization with moral authority. In short, we have largely chosen to see life as tragic rather than comic. But to the extent that you participate in this world view, I believe you are limiting your potential for success in the material sense and—even more importantly—you are doing nothing for your character. Or at least nothing good.

Humor can be your best tool for distancing yourself from the negativity and pessimism that is so rampant at the beginning of the twenty-first century. It's not always an easy tool to use, but I believe it's importance has been seriously underestimated as an element of strong character. George Bernard Shaw said that everything is funny as long as it happens to somebody else. But a really strong person is able to laugh even when the joke's on him. Just as light will conform to various kinds of experiments, if you choose to find humor in life and in your own circumstances, you will find it. If you're of strong enough character to see life as a comedy in the sense I've described, you are strong enough to make it really be that way as well. And I'm quite serious about that!

Thinking Naked—or at Least Thinking in Short Pants

Find a photo of yourself at the age of six or seven. As you look at the picture, try to recapture the thoughts and feelings that defined you at that time of your life. By reconnecting with those feelings, you'll open yourself up to a wide range of new stimuli in the adult world. And that's what thinking naked is all about.

When you were a kid:

What TV shows did you watch?

How did you occupy yourself during the day?

What was your favorite candy?

Who was your best friend?

What did you want to be when you grew up?

What did you most look forward to when you started each day?

Did you have any pets?

What was your favorite sport?

Who was your favorite teacher?

Try to think of more categories that filled up your life in those golden days of yore. What did you enjoy about those things? What do you do now (if anything!) that provides similar satisfaction? And if the answer is "nothing," what can you do to change that? Remember, the more you're able to get into the "think naked" mindset, the closer you'll be to your true self—the person who you really are when nobody's looking.

Seeing Through a Kid's Eyes

During a product development session with Gatorade, I hit upon a way to literally see the world through a kid's eyes. I bought a couple of dozen disposable cameras and passed them out at my son's grade school. The kids were glad to get the free cameras, but they also wanted to know what they were supposed to photograph.

"It's easy," I told them. "Just have fun. Shoot the coolest stuff you can find. Over the next seventy-two hours, take pictures of all the things you like best. Anything and everything. At home, on the street, even off the TV screen if you want. Then we'll develop all the pictures and see what we've got."

When it was over, we had close to 600 photos

of the world according to an eight-year-old. There were pets and Barbies, sports jerseys and rubber monsters. There were even shots of mom and dad. Most interestingly, it turned out that the kids were also deeply into collectibles of all kinds—toys, trading cards and even the packaging of the products. This insight would never have happened without the camera project, which was really a way of getting the kids to think naked and to create a recorded image of their experience. The photos provided great stimulus for creative thinking in our invention sessions for Gatorade. In fact, they were the inspiration for our highest-testing promotional concept.

Long before Bob Dylan was a part of anybody's ad campaign, he used to take a portable radio and a guitar up on the roof of his family's house in Hibbing, Minnesota. Dylan was just little Bobby Zimmerman then, and he didn't have the kind of "good" voice that would lead anybody to suspect that he would ever perform for any audience, much less for the pope. But when Bob was up on the roof trying to pick up Nashville radio stations and playing along with the Grand Ole Opry, he was doing what kids do best. He was thinking naked. He was being an uninhibited child. He didn't become a genius—he already was one, and he just stayed that way.

Ask a Child for Advice

You can take any issue, big or small, and discuss it with a child. You may not want to do exactly what he or she suggests, but you'll definitely get a fresh take on the problem you face. First of all you need to explain it to the child. Sometimes the answer will reveal itself to you as you're explaining it.

THE LOOK THE LOOK THE LOOK

THE LOOK THE LOOK THE LOOK

THE LOOK THE LOOK THE LOOK

THE
THE LOOK THE LOOK
LOOK
THE LOOK THE LOOK

THE LOOK THE LOOK THE LOOK

THE LOOK THE LOOK THE LOOK

THE LOOK THE LOOK THE LOOK

THE LOOK THE LOOK THE LOOK

THE LOOK THE LOOK THE LOOK

THE LOOK THE LOOK THE LOOK

THE LOOK THE LOOK THE LOOK

THE LOOK THE LOOK THE LOOK

THE LOOK THE LOOK THE LOOK

THE LOOK

THE LOOK

THE LOOK

THE LOOK

THE LOOK THE LOOK THE LOOK

THE LOOK THE LOOK THE LOOK

THE LOOK THE LOOK THE LOOK

THE LOOK THE LOOK THE LOOK

SOMETHINGS are easier to recognize than to define. Take "The Look," for instance . . .

A caveman drops his pterodactyl drumstick into the fire. He fishes it out. He takes a bite. He smiles broadly at the other cavemen.

They give him *The Look* . . .

An Egyptian pharaoh announces his intention to build a pyramid, and it's gonna be a big one. Some blocks of stone weighing between two and thirty tons will have to be floated down the Nile on barges, then dragged across the desert, then levered into position with wooden poles. How many blocks? About two million of them, says the pharaoh . . .

He gets *The Look* . . .

A young cartoonist draws a mouse. "Someday this mouse will be the foundation of a billion-dollar company," he tells his wife. "By the way, the mouse's name is Mortimer."

Mrs. Disney rolls her eyes.

Walt gets *The Look* . . .

"Honey, I'll change his name to Mickey!"

But he gets *The Look* again!

The list of Lookers and Lookees could go on and on. At one time or another, I'm certain you've gotten The Look. You've done something or said something that made the room go silent in shock. And early on, you learned to avoid that experience like the plague. But, really, getting The Look can be a very good sign. It means you may be straddling the line between stupidity and genius and you may be onto something distinctive and new.

That's why, in any creative collaboration, it's best to totally reject the idea that any idea should be totally rejected. Start with the assumption that every suggestion, no matter how outlandish, is an opportunity for innovative thinking. If someone's idea is greeted with total incomprehension, make sure the speaker sees this as an encouragement to take the thought even further.

The Look doesn't mean "You're a moron." It's just a spontaneous reaction that can spur you on to creating new neural synapses, more convolutions in the gray matter, and a better brain all around and a more original YOU.

Actually, the opposite of The Look is the true enemy of the creative process. You know you're in trouble when people respond to your wild notions with folded hands and polite nods. That's why it's so important to challenge yourself to take your ideas further—to build on a thought rather than back off. It's about getting past the fear of standing out. Because even if you don't want to be at the center of the stage, that should be a conscious decision, not a reflex motivated by fear. I personally do like to stand out to some extent, and I try hard to do it in the right way. Off the wall but in control. Purposeful defiance but positive impact.

There are some people who break the law and aren't afraid to die in the process. They're definitely willing to stand out, but I wouldn't call them creative individuals. Maybe they want to get The Look, but that's all they want. The Look should be a means to an end. When you get it, you should feel just a twinge of fear—but you don't stop there. You build something positive out of that fear. It's a starting point rather than a stop sign. At the same time, you've got to remember that stop signs do exist, and when you come to one, you stop. A hungry mule will keep eating until his stomach bursts, even if you hit him with a stick trying to make him stop. He's fearless—and foolish—and that's never a good combination.

The truly courageous person is not immune to fear, but it plays a different role in his or her life than it does for other people. If you're a courageous person, your fears aren't about what someone might do to you or something that might happen to you. Your fears are about not living up to your ideals, about reacting instead of acting, and about not taking advantage of the opportunities that are always within your reach.

A truly courageous person is not afraid of what may or may not happen next week or next year. He fears not making the most of every moment today—

A truly courageous person fears the impulse to dominate other people. She leads by helping others to be their best—

A truly courageous person fears doing anything that he or his loved ones might be ashamed of—

A truly courageous person fears making appearances more important than realities—fears making impressions more important than communication—fears making herself more important than people who are depending on her—

But here's the one thing a courageous person fears most. Have you ever seen a deer caught in the headlights of a car? The deer just stands there as though paralyzed, with the car bearing down. The truly courageous person fears ever being like that, and every moment of his or her life is dedicated to making sure it never happens.

In other words the truly courageous person—as Franklin Delano Roosevelt once said—fears nothing except fear itself. It's not fear of getting The Look—it's fear of never getting it!

Just Do It. Really!

I learned how important this is a few years ago while working on a project for Nike. Suddenly an idea came to me: What if there was a shoe just for running fast? A sprinting shoe without the spikes?

At that time, Reebok was having great success with a shoe designed for step training. I knew that whoever had thought of that must have gotten the mother of all The Looks—so I blurted out, "What if Nike owned speed the way Reebok owns step? What if we did a sprinting shoe without the spikes?"

Wow. Within seconds I created twenty expressions

of complete mystification. There was silence. Utter and complete peace and quiet. My face changed color several times.

As we started to create the concepts, a colleague, scrunching his face, said, "Marc, running is distance. Eight miles. Ten miles. Twenty-six miles. It's not sprinting from here to the corner." And I caved. I admit it. What did I say? I think it was, "Homina, homina . . ." Maybe it was, "Yada yada . . ."

Several years later I was watching the NCAA basketball tournament when a Nike commercial came on. An overnight delivery guy, a samurai chef, Olympic sprinter Michael Johnson, and base-stealing specialist Kenny Lofton were shown sitting in an encounter group apologizing for their sheer speed. What made that speed possible—in fact, inevitable!—was a brand new Nike shoe technology called Zoom Air. Lighter, faster, more responsive. Designed especially for sprinting! Built for speed!

As the commercial faded, I made some kind of sound. Maybe a "Rah!" because I had been proven right, but also a "Nah!"—because I had bailed out when I got The Look.

Let your High Concept guide what you say! When your heart and your gut give you a sense of where to go, you may get The Look—and let's hope so!

Practice Getting The Look

1. Right now, think of a problem you're having that involves other people. It doesn't have to be a dire

situation, just something in a personal or profes-
sional relationship that you'd like to change and
improve.

2. Think of something that you could do in this situation that would really shake things up. What can
you do or say that will fundamentally alter the sta-
tus quo? It should definitely make the other parties
uncomfortable. In fact, it should make you uncomfortable too. But it must be with the intention of
making things better, perhaps not immediately,
but certainly over the long term. And it should
come from your personal strategy!

3. Now visualize exactly what you think would happen if you were to act upon the plan you came up
with in step 2. How do you think other people
would react? What would they say? What would
they do? How would you feel if those reactions
were directed your way? How would you react if
you got The Look?

4. Once you've got a clear mental picture of the
probable outcome, write a brief but detailed
description of what will happen. Be sure to include
any feelings you expect to have and the things you
imagine you would say.

5. Finally, put your vision into action in the real
world. Did you get The Look? How does what
really happened compare to what you wrote
down?

WHEN YOU HAVE PASSION, YOU
HAVE PERMISSION   WHEN YOU
HAVE   PASSION,   YOU   HAVE

WHEN YOU HAVE PASSION, YOU HAVE PERMISSION

PERMISSION
PASSION, YOU HAVE PERMISSION
WHEN YOU HAVE PASSION, YOU
HAVE PERMISSION WHEN YOU
HAVE PASSION, YOU HAVE

PERMISSION   WHEN YOU HAVE
PASSION, YOU HAVE PERMISSION
WHEN YOU HAVE PASSION, YOU

WHEN YOU HAVE PASSION, YOU

HAVE PERMISSION WHEN YOU

HAVE PASSION, YOU HAVE

PERM HAVE

PASS SSION

WHE , YOU

HAVI YOU

HAVI HAVE

PERMISSION WHEN YOU HAVE

PASSION, YOU HAVE PERMISSION

WHEN YOU HAVE PASSION, YOU

WHEN YOU'RE faced with a bunch of conventional thinkers, following your heart and standing your ground takes great resilience. But challenging conventional wisdom has its rewards—in your work, in your relationships, in your life.

Anybody can just be an ornery cuss and yell that two plus two makes five, but that's not really very productive. The kind of dissent we'll be discussing in this chapter is something very different. It's proactive! It's positive! It's creative!

Creative dissent occurs when someone goes against the grain with the intention of making things better. It's not just making waves, it's making improvements. The dissent comes from firmly believing that you know a better way. You feel it in your gut.

Creative dissent isn't bucking the system to be a jerk. Its challenging the present state of affairs—questioning things—knowing that from the beginning of time things have always been improved upon, and that they can still be improved even more. The fathers of this country were dissenters, they didn't accept that things were "just that way." Creative dissent occurs at every level in life from politics to relationships to breakfast cereals.

Take people who liked a nice bowl of hot, toasted cereal. It was a very time-consuming process until John Kellogg came up with an idea of precooked cereals that could be poured out of a box into a bowl. He crushed corn and barley malt, rolled it together and baked it in sheets. He then broke the baked sheets into flakes. In 1907, when cereal meant waking up 30 to 45 minutes earlier each morning, Creative Dissenter Kellogg invented the first cold yet wholesome cereal, Corn Flakes, which could be prepared and consumed in a matter of minutes.

When you can make bucking conventional wisdom a reflex instead of just a tactic you use on occasion, you possess the power to achieve greatness. Once you have your High Concept in place, you begin to trust your intuition much more freely. After having referred to your personal roadmap on a regular basis you can almost instantly feel when something is right. This kind of trust in your own intuition can spell tremendous success. Because intuition will defeat intelligence alone every time.

There's an old saying: "If it's not broken, don't fix it." But sometimes your gut will tell you to "break" something on purpose, just to see if something better can be made from the ground up. Whenever I try to do that, I feel that I'm really acting in accordance with my high concept—Purposeful Defiance with Positive Impact.

Of course, a finely tuned gut instinct means you might be the only person who knows that a solution or a path to a solution is the right one for you. You have to stand your ground and allow your passion to dispel whatever doubts you might have. Challenge your internal lemmings. Slay the sacred cows and redirect your thinking.

A highly honed gut instinct is often a creative person's most lethal weapon. In the world of inventing, where you're besieged by the unknown at every turn, your gut instinct is often all you have to go on. Use your High Concept to cultivate your gut instinct, and you can trust in this: When you're faced with a question in a relationship, at work or in life, your "gut reaction" will often guide you to the place you need to be.

Ask for Forgiveness, Not Permission

When your High Concept tells you that you're on the right track, go for it! The effort it takes to convince other people that what you're doing will work is often a big waste of time and energy. More often than not, it's better to just keep your focus and make whatever you're doing happen than to check to make sure it's okay to try it. This isn't to say we're bucking the system or just plowing through. It's that in order to get permission, you'll have to get off the highway, make a call, get a busy signal—and possibly lose the opportunity forever.

Not that you should disregard authority and just charge ahead with something without concern for the consequences—that would be stupid. Quite frankly, anyone can run off wildly and do what he or she feels is right without regard for a given framework. But what's the point? The reality in life is that we seldom make the rules. We must use our inventive minds to work within them, stretch them and potentially make new rules, rules that allow for constant improvement.

How can you turn this into a personal strategy? Think about it. The next time any issue pops up that has two or more outcomes, pay attention to your gut feeling, your passion. I'm not telling you to act on it, but I am telling you to pay attention to the First Gut Instinct.

Uncommon Sense

How many times have you heard someone described as "street smart," or as having a lot of "common sense." "She isn't that smart, but she has common sense." Common sense typically leads you toward good, safe alternatives. Use your common sense, and conventional solutions are right around the corner. But what about this notion of uncommon sense, when the rules are clearly stated and somehow someone finds a loophole? Sometimes life offers you opportunities because you have uncommon sense. The essence of being inventive means that you've come up with something that is uncommon. No one has seen it before, and more than likely no one has thought of it! Damn, that frustrates the rule makers! There is no better example of an uncommon thinker than former Cincinnati Bengals coach Sam Wyche.

Sam Wyche, TV sports analyst, is a fiery man, full of great intentions but, nonetheless, fiery. If he believes in something, forget about it—he has to follow his heart. As the coach of the Cincinnati Bengals in the '80s, his fiery no-holds-barred attitude would sometimes get him in some hot water. He was always true to his own High Concept, so you would sometimes see his mercury rise if someone from the press challenged his wisdom. They said he had no common sense when he'd call certain plays. What Sam Wyche had was Uncommon Sense, uncommon because what Sam did in his coaching career was "buck the trend" when things made no sense! When the lemmings were all going to the right, Sam always looked to the left. He is perhaps best known as the inventor of the No-Huddle offense, a reflexive action that his Bengals would take, all within the rules of the game.

In their 1990 campaign toward the Super Bowl, Sam's Bengals would sometimes not employ the common practice of retreating seven yards behind the line of scrimmage to call their next play; instead, they'd stand on the line of scrimmage, watch what defense the other team was going to employ and call a play at the line. Wait a minute! This infuriated other coaches, and the NFL front office was at a loss for words because Sam Wyche in his uncommon sense of wisdom had figured out how to get a tactical advantage over his opponents within the confines of the rules! All his detractors wanted his head on a platter! All his detractors, mostly coaches from other teams, started to figure out how his system worked and quickly employed it themselves! Sam Wyche, Creative Dissenter, making something better within the confines of the rules, showed us that every rule, with some modification, can be truly enlightening.

When You Have Passion, You Have Permission

Sometimes when your creative dissent escalates, not only do you see something that nobody else can see, but you start to feel so impassioned about it that you couldn't live with yourself if you didn't see it through. These are the times when you must express your true self, because only then will you gain the power to truly move the world. You have passion, a human characteristic that has led people to discover continents, ignited love affairs, and inspired art, music and literature. You have what the forefathers of this nation had when they created the Constitution. You have what Romeo had for Juliet, what Siegfried has for Roy. When you have passion, you have permission.

In Italy the passionate embrace of two lovers doesn't even get a second look; instead, it is expected! When you feel strongly about music, art, love, soccer, life, you should say it loud and proud. Passion and hope are what drives life—the rewards are incredible.

To have loved intensely and lost is not just better than never to have loved at all. It's actually one of the best experiences life can offer because it has stretched your capacity to live.

> *Senza la speranza non che la vita.*
> (Without hope there is no life.)
> —Maria Marsan, my mamma

Passion allows you the opportunity to jump in with both feet, without regard for the possibility of injury or ridicule. Passion drives us all to great things; when you feel it down to your last fiber, passion can blind you, make you unaware of potential danger. But it's also the means by which greatness is achieved!

Don't ever let yourself be sidetracked when you have passion. You may fail, but if you believed in something, down to your very core and you made it happen with abandon, that is total honor. How much did you learn about yourself in those situations? What new inspirations did you experience? How did you grow? In what direction did you evolve?

Personal story time! Have you ever been in love right down to the center of your bones, to the point where it accompanied your thoughts every minute of every day? So much in love that you redefined what you would do for someone, that your passion drove you to new heights and most assuredly to new lows. That's the Danger Zone, where poetry flows from your heart, where a monthly delivery of flowers would mark the anniversary of the day you met, where singing a song written on a napkin, with musical accompaniment, in a crowded restaurant is done without batting an eye!

Gulp! I was there . . . I was driven by total passion—sure I was incoherent at times, but it felt so honorable, it was so undeniable, and it redefined me forever. My capacity for love, communication, self-expression changed forever by virtue of this incredible relationship. I felt like a fourth grader again; in my mind I was running around as I had on the playgrounds of my youth, full of excitement and anticipation. The relationship was defined by this "happy tension," this deliciously sweet yet dangerous place, where the stakes are high and you have the possibility of one of two extremes—incredible passion and joy . . . or a crippled heart. We all go there, and most of us don't like to know that we could get burned big time, but it's definitely the Danger Zone. Here's the rub: The Danger Zone, when entered without reservation, without thought of injury, entered with total abandon, can redefine you. In fact, it's where I choose to be in life. I don't ever want my emotions deadened, like nerve endings gone bad with life's barrage of negatives. I want to live each and every day with the thought, "With passion comes enormous joy and possible pain—and the pain in most cases will either kill you if you allow it to or make you great!" I mean really great both in the eyes of your peers and in your own!

The deeper that sorrow carves into your being, the more joy you can contain. Is not the cup that holds your wine the very cup that was burned in the potter's oven? And is not the lute that soothes your spirit the very wood that was hollowed with knives?

When you are joyous, look deep into your heart and you shall find it is only that which has given you sorrow that is giving you joy. When you are sorrowful look again in your heart and you shall see that in truth you are weeping for that which has been your delight.

—From *The Prophet,* by Kahlil Gibran

When you see something, when you really get a vision of what's in front of you and no one else can see it, stick with it, and don't let anyone convince you to do otherwise. This is a feeling you've got deep in your gut! Ask yourself, do I believe in this person, in this job, in this marriage—I mean right down to the bones! If the answer is yes, than jump in with both feet, with passion and without reservation. Don't wait for something to go wrong or for someone to do what you'd expect them to do. Commit yourself with passion. You have permission!

ANTENNAE UP! ANTENNAE UP!

ANTENNAE UP! ANTENNAE UP!

ANTENNAE UP! ANTENNAE UP!

ANTENNAE UP!

ANTENNAE UP! ANTENNAE UP!

ANTENNAE UP! ANTENNAE UP!

ANTENNAE UP! ANTENNAE UP!

ANTENNAE UP! ANTENNAE UP!

ANTENNAE UP! ANTENNAE UP!

ANTENNAE UP! ANTENNAE UP!

ANTENNAE UP! ANTENNAE UP!

ANTENNAE UP! ANTENNAE UP!

ANTENNAE UP! ANTENNAE UP!

ANTENNAE UP! ANTENNAE UP!

ANT UP!

ANT UP!

ANT UP!

ANT UP!

ANTENNAE UP! ANTENNAE UP!

ANTENNAE UP! ANTENNAE UP!

ANTENNAE UP! ANTENNAE UP!

ANTENNAE UP! ANTENNAE UP!

POLLY MATZINGER is an outstanding trainer of Border collies. Her dogs can herd sheep with the best of them. But that's only one part of Polly's life, and the other part would seem to be about as far from sheep herding as you can get. Polly Matzinger is also a world-class authority on the human immune system and uses of immunology in medical issues such as cancer and organ transplants. Dr. Matzinger is chief of the T Cell Tolerance and Memory Section in a division of the National Institute of Health. One of her major research objectives is to explain why the immune system fails to consistently attack cancer cells. Why doesn't the body react to tumor growth with the defenses that it uses against other forms of disease? This would seem to be a question best investigated in a laboratory, with a microscope, slides and a row of petrie dishes. But Polly Matzinger's most recent hypotheses about the immune system are derived from watching her dogs herd and protect flocks of sheep. She's convinced that it's the fright of the sheep that alerts dogs to the presence of an intruder—not the intruder itself. Can this insight translate into more effective cancer treatment? According to Dr. Francesco Marincola of the National Cancer Institute, "Correct or not, Matzinger's theory is an historic intellectual step. No theory is better for the moment than hers." And, correct or not, Polly Matzinger is a true practitioner of the principle we'll explore in this chapter. It's called *Antennae Up!*

Where do great ideas come from? Where can you find insights and inspirations to transform your life? How can you make something great even better?

The short answer is: almost anywhere—but you do need to go out into the world with your antennae up and your attention set on "search." Your intention is to find a stimulus that shakes you out of your old patterns. You need to gather new information . . . challenge your mind . . . expand your spirit . . . change the way you look at every aspect of your life. Even small alterations can make a big difference when you're really committed to the creative self-growth. Because you never know when an acorn is going to turn into an oak tree, and it can happen faster than you think . . .

One day an Oxford University mathematics professor named Charles Dodgson took the young daughters of a colleague for a ride in a rowboat. The girls wanted to hear a story, so the professor invented one. It was such a good story that the girls insisted he write it out for them. *Alice's Adventures in Wonderland* was born . . .

Around the same time, an insurance salesman had just lost his business. Again and again, he had failed to get signed documents from potential clients—he never had a pen handy. Out of this adversity came the inspiration for a deceptively complex writing instrument. Edward Waterman called it the fountain pen . . .

Roughly a hundred years later, a man named Ed Sobek was having trouble finding opponents for his favorite sports of tennis and squash. He was simply too good a player. But what if there were a game that was so easy to play that even novices could quickly attain competitive levels? Ed Sobek took the felt covering off a tennis ball, sawed off the handle of a tennis racquet, and whacked the ball against the wall of a handball court. Today, the game of racquetball is played by millions of people worldwide . . .

A great novel was inspired by an afternoon boat ride. A breakthrough creation grew from financial catastrophe. A popular new sport was created because someone couldn't find a tennis game. Lives—and the world—are transformed because of random coincidence . . . dire need . . . or just because someone says, "Why the hell not?" Great ideas can happen at any time, in any setting.

Or almost any setting. There are a couple of very important exceptions.

The fact is, great ideas rarely come from perfectly quiet rooms with the phone off the hook, a sheet of blank paper in front of you and a well-sharpened pencil in your hand.

Real creation almost never happens when someone (even if it's yourself) says, "You'd better come up with something good—or else!"

Breakthrough thinking almost never takes place when you're racking your brain in an environment that's tailor-made for brain racking.

In those situations, the gears of the human mind go metal-on-metal, fruitlessly grinding and turning, as you contemplate the dead fly on the windowsill. This sort of ritualized groping for ideas is known as "mind grind." And it hurts!

Mind Grind

The mind grind environment is very hostile to creative thinking—but how do you avoid it? After all, you want soooo badly to lead the fulfilling life every human being deserves, but the more you want it, the more you try, the more you struggle, the more you pound the table and gnash your teeth, why, the more your mind grinds, damn it!

Fortunately, there are many ways out of this dilemma. In fact, life is full of opportunities for conditioning your mind differently. Some of them are easy, and others are more challenging. Some of them are like a mind massage. Others are what I call a "Brain Wedgie," when reality sneaks up behind you and says, "How do you like this, big shot?" The really important thing is to take advantage of anything that shakes you out of the mind grind rut, even if it's a couple of hours of doing exactly what you want, rather than what you're "supposed" to be doing.

Are you nodding your head in agreement? I'm saying you should take a walk in the park near your house, right? Or listen to your favorite music. Or read a book you've always loved. Or pet the neighbor's dog—and then you'll feel better, won't you?

Well, not exactly. You might feel warm and fuzzy if you do those things, but you probably won't feel more creative. Or more inspired. All those activities are just too easy. They're just too deep inside your well-worn comfort zone.

Really positive stimulus always includes an element of challenge. So challenge your senses. Challenge your mind. Challenge the neighborhood bully to step outside!

Instead of taking a walk in the park near your house, take a walk in the park across town. Listen to music you've never heard before. Read a new book. Pet a frog, not a dog. Dogs get plenty of petting. The frog might turn into a prince! (Or a princess, if you prefer.) As Kurt Vonnegut put it, "Do one thing every day that scares you."

Psychologists refer to a mindset known as functional fixedness, in which any problem is approached with a low-risk, low-reward orientation. Another term for this condition might be psychosclerosis—or hardening of the attitudes!

When you stimulate yourself intellectually and emotionally, you create new mental pathways to counter psychosclerosis. Research supports this.

DO AS THE MANKATO NUNS DO AND MAKE INVENTING A HABIT!

For example, 700 nuns living in Mankato, Minnesota, are the largest group of brain donors in the world. Their average age is eighty-five, and twenty-five of them are older than ninety.

Compared to the general population, the Mankato nuns suffer less frequently from dementia, Alzheimer's, or other debilitating conditions. Why? Researchers believe it's because they refuse to let their minds sit still. The elderly sisters make mental stimulation part of their daily lives. They study new languages, learn how to play musical instruments, and stay active through volunteer work. By donating their brains to science, the Mankato nuns are helping scientists examine the effects of lifelong stimulation on mental health.

.   .   .

While it's true that exciting things can happen to you during a plain old walk around the block, or even a plain old walk to your television set, your chances are a lot better if you actively look for situations that jog your mind. It's all a matter of seeking out what I call strategic stimulus.

Why "strategic"? Because this is part of the larger plan you have for yourself. It's a tool you consciously use for moving yourself forward. Strategic stimulus is not an accident. You make it happen. You deliberately put yourself in the track of inspiration so it can roll over you like a runaway locomotive. Now that's an epiphany!

But be warned: strategic stimulus demands some discrimination. We live in the most hyped-up, communication-saturated era the world has known. Cell phones, Web sites, satellite dishes—it's easy to become a multitasking fool. So don't just gorge yourself on mental stimuli. Seek out stimuli that nourish you and help you grow, not stimuli that simply wash over your back.

A strategic stimulus doesn't always slam you right between the eyes. Often, finding it requires scanning the periphery. You've got to look from side to side instead of merely straight ahead.

Here's how former Senator Bill Bradley describes the process:

> When I was a kid, I used to walk down the street, then stop by a shop window. With my head still facing down the street, I'd say to myself, I can see that red blouse in the window. I can see that pair of black shoes. Once, during my first week as a pro basketball player, I ran across the street against the light. Out of the corner of my eye, I suddenly saw a car speeding right at me, and I had just enough time to jump. I came out of it with a bruised hip and wrist, but at least I didn't get run over. I remember thinking, "Thank God for my peripheral vision." Practicing peripheral vision also led me to the discovery that I could look one way on the basketball court and see things other players couldn't. That made it easier for me to pass

or move. This way of seeing the game naturally led to the idea of its being a sort of radar in life or your profession, constantly scanning all the possible implications for any particular action. My eyes have become a metaphor for a frame of mind.

Your Wants, Your Needs, Your Plans for Action

Wherever there is a desire or a need, there is also an opportunity to maximize. You can learn to use your own needs to ignite your creative spirit and inspire you to action.

Now, in the exercises below, we'll focus on identifying strategic stimuli that can help you achieve your goals.

Goals and Strategic Stimuli

In each of the two columns below there is a blank space for your objectives in reading this book. The objectives can be life goals or what needs to be accomplished this very week. Spend some time thinking about each of the objectives. What are the resources that can help you? Who are the DNAs that can offer consultation? Enter this information along with other forms of strategic stimulus you can use!

Example Objective: To become a better parent

Strategic Stimulus (Thinking Naked): Try to become a peer with your child, read what they

are reading, listen to their music, play with
them. Keep a diary on what you do together.

Strategic Stimulus (Get The Look): Get the phone
numbers or e-mail addresses for the greatest
parents on earth. Mrs. Brady? Barbara Bush?
Cheng and Eng? And have a monthly powwow,
solicit their advice, exchange parenting tips.

Strategic Stimulus: Test your High Concept for a
day with your children and see if you feel more
directed as a parent. If not, rewrite your High
Concept.

Objective #1:   Objective #2:

_____   _____

_____   _____

_____   _____

Strategic Stimulus: Strategic Stimulus:

_____   _____

_____   _____

_____   _____

_____   _____

_____   _____

_____   _____

_____   _____

_____   _____

_____   _____

Your Inspiration Inventory

Among the things that inspire me are the movie *Braveheart*, my son's smile, the city of Florence, and my Italian immigrant parents. What inspires you?

People who inspire you! (famous or not)

1. _____

2. _____

3. _____

4. _____

5. _____

Places that inspire you (real or imagined)

1. _____
   _____

2. _____
   _____

3. _____
   _____

4. _____
   _____

5. _____
   _____

Events that touched your heart, mind and soul
(these may be personal, public or historical)

1. _____

_____

_____

_____

2. _____

_____

_____

_____

3. _____

_____

_____

_____

4. _____

_____

_____

_____

5. _____

_____

_____

_____

What worries you? What are the things that keep you up at night? What are your biggest fears? Are you worried about losing your job? Are you afraid your lover is losing interest? Do you worry about getting home in time for a TV show?

Write down the top five worries that come to mind.

1. _____

_____

_____

_____

2. _____

_____

_____

_____

3. _____

_____

_____

_____

4. _____

_____

_____

_____

5. _____

_____

_____

_____

And now for something completely different. What makes you smile? What makes you laugh? In fact, what are the five funniest things you can think of right now? Whether they're situations you've been in, jokes you've heard, or just ideas that have crossed your mind, write down the top five.

1. _____

_____

_____

_____

2. _____

_____

_____

_____

3. _____

_____

_____

_____

4. _____

_____

_____

_____

5. _____

_____

_____

_____

None of us likes to admit it, but sometimes we're inspired or driven by someone who didn't believe in us—someone who became our personal brick wall, someone who just didn't get it. Was there someone who could have helped you but instead they got in the way, became antagonistic, became a toxic footnote in your life? Wouldn't it be great to thumb your nose at them, burn their shorts or just plain prove that they were wrong about you? Who were these naysayers in your life, and what were the events that will be forever linked to their memory?

Your Brain: Give It Dimension, Texture and "Flava"

When it comes to taking up your personal game, hatching new ideas, and solving prickly problems, why settle for just your own knowledge and experience? Instead, talk to someone whose knowledge and experience can help you—someone with a different DNA. Because it's very difficult to solve problems in isolation.

Using many DNAs for problem solving is smart. So consult the experts. Want to get a better idea of your spirituality? Attend the worship services of half a dozen religious denominations. Want to learn more about your teenage son or daughter? Go to a mosh pit on Friday night or to a video games arcade. Want to better understand your four-year-old? Take a seat on a park bench right next to a sandbox. Sometimes you don't even have to talk to an expert. All you need to do is "watch an expert."

Don't let other people make up your mind for you, but do pay serious attention to differing points of view. Asking for help is never a sign of weakness— it's a sign of strength and intelligence.

Create a DNA Hit Squad

Your DNA Hit Squad is a group of people you can rely on for strategic stimulus whenever you feel the need. The Hit Squad can consist of friends, family members or coworkers in any combination, as long as the group possesses a divergent collection of DNA. The key is finding people who have unique knowledge in all the areas of your life that you wish to develop.

For example, I want to be:

1. **Spiritually aware**—so I listen to Father Larry Tharp. Larry is one of the few Catholic priests who makes going to church fun and enlightening in equal part, or I talk to Arun Prabhu about Hinduism and his personal journey to spiritual enlightenment.

2. **On the edge**—so I go out with my friend Ann who has been known to say "I'll try anything once."

3. **Youthful**—so I call my twenty-two-year-old cousin, Andrea, and ask for recommendations on music, cool Web-sites, reading materials, issues of the day.

4. **Simple and insightful**—so when I want an honest assessment, one that cuts right to the chase, I talk to my mom or my ten-year-old son. They seem to get to the heart of a problem and offer useful no-nonsense advice every time.

5. **Fun-loving**—People like Chris Taylor and Gary Kopervas make me "gut laugh." I love the feeling of being worn out by laughter.

6. **Pure all the way through**—I love people who show you what they are and who are what they show you. People who are just a little bit cocky but who can back it up. My good friend Mitch is like that. During the late 1950s he wrestled

professionally around Pontiac, Michigan, using the name Duke Rhino—and today he's an ordained rabbi. Mitch definitely has chutzpah.

Choose Your DNA Hit Squad

Who would you choose to be on your DNA Hit Squad? Who would you want on your Joint Chiefs of Staff, your trusted group of advisors, your personal DNA/stimulus committee? Each of your selections should contribute a unique point of view, because your Team ought to be a microcosm of the world. Write their names in the spaces below and what each brings to you in terms of new and meaningful perspective:

1. _____

2. _____

3. _____

4. _____

5. _____

Last Year's Surprises

These are more often than not things that you originally thought you wouldn't do but did—and you wound up finding out something valuable about yourself in the process. They're growth experiences, both big and small. Use the provided space to review some of those surprise moments that occurred during the past twelve months.

Your VCR (Visions, Choices, Resolutions)

What if your life were a videocassette and you had the ability to rewind and fast-forward at will. You'd have the ability to conjure up more choices about your life today by looking back into your past or fast-forwarding into your future. By having more choices, you'd stand a better chance of resolving the situation you are in today.

Use "fast forward" to help you resolve a particularly troublesome situation that you're faced with right now, using your proactive and positive responses to the situation. Fast-forward one year, then five years, then ten years. At each interval think of what the situation will look like. How will this situation ultimately resolve itself? Say it out loud and then write it down. Use the first space provided to write down the current situation and the second space to write down how it will resolve itself.

Current situation:

_____

_____

_____

_____

_____

_____

_____

_____

_____

_____

Fast-forward. How it will resolve itself?

_____

_____

_____

_____

_____

_____

_____

_____

_____

This technique can work both ways. By "rewinding," you could think of a difficult situation you were in several years ago, perhaps one that occupied your every thought. Think of the steps you've been through that have brought you to your current, more stable resolution. Is there anything that you could have done differently that would have brought about an easier resolution?

Former situation:

_____

_____

_____

_____

_____

_____

_____

_____

_____

_____

How was it resolved?

_____

_____

_____

_____

_____

_____

_____

_____

_____

_____

_____

How could it have happened differently?

_____

_____

_____

_____

_____

_____

_____

_____

_____

_____

_____

Health Food for the Brain

A creative brain is one that searches out input, insights and intelligence other than its own. It feeds on surprises.

Gathering stimuli that include differing points of view challenges you to rethink long-held biases, moth-eaten perspectives or crusty beliefs. Searching out stimuli challenges you to make forced associations you wouldn't normally make and can spark new connections between "idea links."

Forced associations between seemingly unrelated people, places or things help your mind become a lean, mean thinking machine. Variety may be the spice of life, but stimuli are the essence of inventing, and inventing a great life comes from keeping your eyes open.

As long as there is a need, there's the need to create. As long as there is a world full of stimuli at your beck and call, you will have a way to realize your dreams. You will be able to create the very best you.

Peeling the Onion

Write down your High Concept and peel away the elements in order to find a constant source of improvement. It's a matter of thinking carefully about the elements of your concept and also of calling up their various associations. Here's how this works for me with my High Concept.

My High Concept:
Purposeful defiance with positive impact

Purposeful:
Like the waves of the ocean destined for a shore
Like the wondering eyes of a child
Like a squirrel looking for food in winter
Like Lee Majors when he starred in three TV series

Defiance:
Like Tommie Smith when he raised his fist in
     protest in the 1968 Summer Olympic Games
Like Dr. Henry Heimlich when detractors told
     him his maneuver was not medically sound

Like the forefathers of any revolution who truly
  had the interests of the people in mind

Like Abraham Lincoln

Positive Impact:

Like a hammer hitting a nail just right

Like helping to raise money to cure a terrible disease

Like making someone smile

Like truly respecting people

A Brain Chain Reaction

You have an idea. Let's look at it scientifically. Your
idea is nothing more than an electrical impulse that's
transmitted by the neurons in your brain. It can
spark another impulse that can spark a third. And a
fourth. In fact, your idea can set off a chain reaction
of impulses that can light up your brain like a switch-
board. We'll call this a brain chain reaction.

Once you learn how to exercise your "brain chain
reflex," you can develop new thoughts and ideas by
linking them to one another.

Here's how it works . . .

Idea Links: The Stuff Brainstorms
Are Made of

Most great ideas usually come from lots of smaller
ideas. Computers. The telephone. The paper diaper.
New-to-the-world ideas don't usually come fully

formed in a single bolt from the blue. They happen with round after round of refining and recombining ideas. Brain chains!

An inventive thinker understands that an idea is only part of a bigger idea. So it's up to you to condition yourself to think of an idea as a means to an end. One idea usually won't get you to where you're going. Think of every small idea as a stepping stone along the path. Remember the High Concept chapter when we went through a number of different exercises that revealed possible High Concepts. They were in essence individual idea links, when we string them together and make them seamless (In a sentence, poem, catchy phrase). BOOM! That's when you've created a strong High Concept.

How Do You Start a Brain Chain?

Brain chains sometimes start with a rough idea or a gut reaction to a problem: "Sales on our widget have dropped," or "Boy, I like Sally." And sometimes they start with a simple, straightforward question that sets things off, like "What could we do to promote this year's model of widget?" or "What could I do to get Sally's attention?"

As ideas start springing up, you need to consider each one at its face value. Explore each idea as it pops up. Give it some room to breathe and expand. Take it a step or two further. Ask yourself, "What if we did this to it" or "Why not do this with it?"

Don't throw anything away, and don't reject anything. Send your critic out of the room. He can come back later.

Look at each idea as an idea link on its way to becoming a bigger and better idea. And it isn't a "good" or a "bad" idea. It just "IS." Spend some time with it. Get to know each idea. Understand its potential. Understand where it can take you.

What Does a Brain Chain Look Like?

A brain chain is a visual representation of you "thinking something through." It charts your brain's processing of a thought or idea. The end result looks like a periodic chart with circles strung together with little lines.

Let's take a shot at brain chaining. All it takes is an open mind, with no barriers, no judgment, only the desire to enhance and improve on a stimulus. Here's an example of brain chaining with "LOVE":

> Love
>
> Tenderness
>
> Poetry
>
> Flowers
>
> 1-800-Flowers
>
> Singing under her/his window
>
> Giving unconditional love
>
> Smiling
>
> Hugging

Sometimes you're the only one that sees something, and the only way to reveal it to the world will be via a brain chain . . . like a translation . . . so that people can understand. That was true with the world's first odometer.

In the first century B.C., for example, Vitruvius invented the world's first odometer. It fit on a horse-drawn carriage and was made up of two gears. When the gears cranked out 5,000 feet (a Roman mile), through one revolution of the 400 teeth of each gear, a stone would drop into a box. One rock, one Roman mile! Over the course of a journey one could count the number of stones and figure out the number of miles traveled. But nobody except Vitruvius could figure out what the hell he was talking about.

400 teeth? 5,000 feet? Wha???

It wasn't until Leonardo Da Vinci came along hundreds of years later, made some sketches, added some insights, and improved Vitruvius's designs that suddenly everybody went, "Duh, oh, yeah! It's an odometer! Hey, what a great idea!" Without Leonardo's brain chain, many more years would have passed without this important tool for travel and measurement.

Brainchain vs. the Clock

Working against tight deadlines for his comic strip, Gary Kopervas regularly needs ideas he can quickly turn into a finished comic strip. Enter the brain chain. Gary will often randomly poke his finger into Webster's dictionary or pull two words out of thin air and brain chain them to see where it leads. One Saturday afternoon, Gary decided to concentrate on the words *animals* and *sports*.

Here's what it looked like.

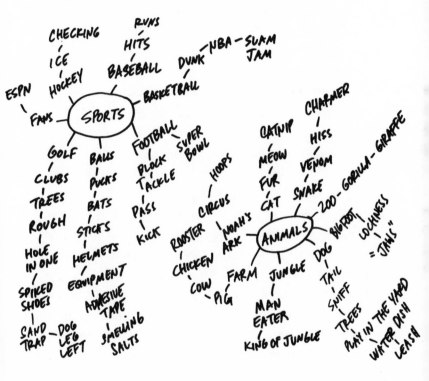

After looking over the words that popped up, Gary focused on the words *dog* and *golf* and brain chained them. And here's the cartoon that came out of it all.

OUT ON A LIMB by GARY KOPERVAS

Another brainchain example:

Success—Resume—Paycheck—Work smarter—
Saving a higher amount per paycheck—
Homes—Maids—Cars—Relationships—
Parenting—Getting things done

Get it? Brain chaining is a snap, but it's got to be a reflex. You have to want to improve, enhance something. Reserve judgment, and build a bigger idea. Now what if you are in a room full of thinkers, different DNAs, and you are all presented with the same problem. WOW! Look out for the fireworks —the number of ideas increases exponentially. Brain chaining can set off those fireworks for you. This is so important, because most of us are too quick to limit our options in life. When you employ this tactic, you can overcome that tendency. Academic studies have always proven that the *quantity* of choices is directly related to the *quality* of the outcome.

Create some brain chains of your own with the following words:

Desire • Explore • Honest • Love • Success

Now use your new skill with some of your possible High Concepts from earlier in the book, create some brain chains:

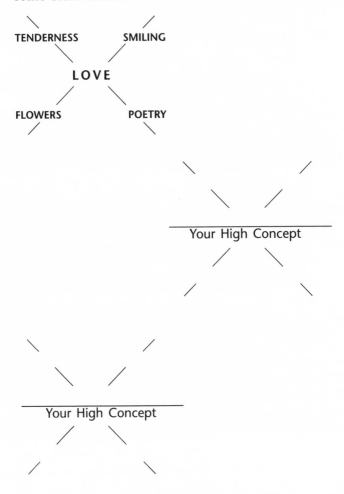

TENDERNESS   SMILING

L O V E

FLOWERS   POETRY

Your High Concept

Your High Concept

FILL THE SPACE! FILL THE
SPACE! FILL THE SPACE! FILL
THE SPACE! FILL THE SPACE!
FILL THE ~~FILL THE SPACE~~ LL THE
SPACE! ~~SPACE~~ PACE! FILL
THE SPACE! FILL THE SPACE!
FILL THE SPACE! FILL THE
SPACE! FILL THE SPACE! FILL
THE SPACE! FILL THE SPACE!
FILL THE SPACE! FILL THE
SPACE! FILL THE SPACE! FILL

FILL THE SPACE! FILL THE SPACE! FILL THE SPACE! FILL THE PACE! FILL . THE SPAC FILL THE PACE! FILL . THE SPACE! FILL THE SPACE! FILL THE SPACE! FILL THE SPACE! FILL THE SPACE! FILL THE SPACE! FILL THE SPACE! FILL

DO YOU wait until a few days before Christmas to finish buying gifts? Or even to start buying them? In college, did you burn the midnight oil to finish the paper you'd had weeks to write? Join the club. It's human nature to put things off until the last minute. Face it, we often work best when we have a deadline. And, uh, each of us does have a deadline—we just don't know exactly when it is.

Shortly before the author William Saroyan passed away, he said, "I always knew people died, but I thought there would be an exception in my case." No exceptions, Bill! This means you . . . and you . . . and you . . . and yes, even you! We're all going to cross over into the great beyond, but that realization can be a very valuable asset once you understand it correctly.

For thousands of years people focused on the afterlife as the most important aspect of human mortality. Once the final gong sounded, would you find yourself sitting on a cloud with a harp in your hands? Or would you go to the Bad Place, where telemarketers are constantly calling, your income tax is always due, and gas costs more than three dollars a gallon? Hey, instead of stressing about life in the great beyond, we should let that ticking clock that's built into each of us call our attention to the present!

How can you make the most of the day that you're living right now? *How can you make the most of the next five minutes?*

Learning to make those questions part of your daily interaction with the world is what I call *filling the space*—not just getting through the days and weeks and years but filling them up with thoughts and feelings and deeds that really matter. Face it, there are certain things you definitely will not be asked about as you await entrance at the pearly gates. There will be no questions about your investment portfolio or your fashion sense. How well did you succeed in making the most of the time you were given? How did you try to help others? How generously did you give love to those around you, and how graciously did you accept their love in return?

Sounds corny, but it's true, folks. Saint Peter has a very corny sensibility. You know those sentimental paintings of the kids with great big eyes? His office is full of 'em. So fill the space, and there's a lot of it to fill. There's plenty of space for all kinds of toys and possessions and stocks that go though the roof, but there's *too much* space for just those things. And the clock is ticking!

There's a commercial for a brand of frozen pizza that shows a man standing before a firing squad. As the riflemen stand at the ready and the drumroll fills the air, a French general addresses the poor guy with a question: "So what would you like on your tombstone?"—the standard last request afforded any condemned man. After a dramatic pause, the man replies, "Extra cheese and pepperoni." Yuk, yuk! While the whimsical commercial was obviously made to sell Tombstone frozen pizza, it raises a very important question. *When you pass onto the great beyond, how do you want people to remember you?*

Admittedly, the question can't be answered off the top of your head, but it's surprising how many people ever think about it. So here's your chance.

Imagine for a moment that you've gone on to your great reward. How do you think people will remember you? What are the specific things you've done that you imagine will stand out in the minds of those who knew you? Right now, are you expressing the human characteristics for which you want to be remembered? Right now, are you the person you want to be?

And when you're done thinking about that, give some thought to the things you *could* have done that you wish people would remember you for. To help you along, try this exercise. Think of things you wish you'd done in each category:

The Things You Didn't Do Exercise

Vacations

_____

_____

Relationships

_____

_____

Work

_____

_____

Starting your own business

_____

_____

Telling someone off

_____

_____

Spreading good cheer

_____

_____

Having more sex

_____

_____

Having less sex

_____

_____

Having just the right amount of sex
   for your height and weight

_____

_____

Upon reflection, do you feel you did something meaningful with your life? Did you have a meaningful effect on someone else's life? Did you leave a legacy? Did you accomplish all that you wanted to while on earth? If you answered "no" to any of these questions, don't fret. The good news is, you're still alive!

Life is what happens when you're busy making other plans.

—John Lennon

Fra dire e fare sta in menze il mare.
(Between saying it and doing it, there is an ocean.)

—Maria Marsan, my mamma

Mo-men-tum

Ultimately, even a big fish gets worn down by swimming upstream all the time. The same thing happens to people who spend their lives going against the current. Since the stream has an enormous amount of power and force, why fight the power? Instead, redirect the power and put it to positive use.

In judo and other martial arts, this is precisely the point. When someone attacks you, you use their momentum to help toss them across the room. The key is avoiding the obvious path of resistance and simply going with the flow.

For example, suppose you wanted to get 46,000 people to dance a Guinness world record dance.

Well, you could start from scratch and get them all to one location, with a band, a sound system, and plenty of advertising. Get them a bunch of incentives, and make sure you get an accurate head count . . .

OR . . .

. . . you could think of a time when 100,000 people are already gathered in one place. Like Oktoberfest 1992 in Cincinnati, Ohio, where there's a bunch of fun-loving partygoers who would dance to anything.

That's the way you make things happen, take the momentum from a situation and redirect it for a bigger payoff! I produced a world record chicken dance in 1992! (I know . . . whoopee!)

How can you get good at "feeling the momentum" of a situation, a relationship or an opportunity. Can this skill help you take shortcuts to answers?

Your Brain Is a Muscle, So Go Ahead and Flex It

Pasko Rakic, a Yale neurobiologist, says it is never too early for children to exercise their minds. Teachers of music and linguistics marvel at a child's ability to learn. Rakic explains, "Children's brains can make far more synaptic connections than can adults'. Shortly after birth the brain makes connections at an incredible pace. There is an ability to learn quickly

in childhood which is unparalleled. As puberty approaches, the number of connections tapers off, the brain starts to eliminate the connections that are not useful and settles on the connections that are. As a teenager, your mental makeup is similar to that of an adult."

Here are some ways you can keep your mental muscle fit and active:

- Do puzzles, challenging ones, do them everyday or do them quickly.

- Learn to play any musical instrument. Albert Einstein played the violin to chill out.

- Do something artistic. Winston Churchill was known to paint. He wasn't great, but it developed a dimension he would otherwise never have known.

- Learn to dance. Do the swing, the hustle, mambo, merengue. You'll be amazed at your raised level of confidence, style and rhythm.

- Date provocative people—better yet, marry one!

A Quick Review

Now that we're almost at the end of the book, I'm going to make an outrageous suggestion. Please read the book a second time! Keep it close by. Make it your palm pilot for the pressing issues of your life. Use the various chapters as reference points for dealing with specific circumstances. For example:

- If you feel you don't have a clear understanding of what direction you want to go in life, review the material on *DNA,* as well as *Nature, Nurture and Navigation.*

- If you don't have a personal mission statement or you want to adjust your present one, read about *High Concept.* It's the most important lesson in this book!

- If you suspect you're becoming way too serious and unimaginative, read *Think Naked!*

- If you find yourself resisting the impulse to challenge the conventional wisdom, take a look at *The Look.*

- If you've become ambivalent about realizing your dreams, look at *When You Have Passion You Have Permission.*

- If you know your direction in life and want to follow it as effectively as possible, read *Antennae Up!*

- If you find yourself putting things off or compromising on the issues that are really important to you, review *Fill the Space!*

Most importantly, remember that the way to do anything substantial is to make it a way of life—a *reflex,* not a *tactic.* The purpose of this book has been to help you create stronger reflexes for life and for living. This can't just be a soup du jour approach to better living. You need to be inventive each day.

Work on your High Concept. Make it lyrical, easy to say, sing it out loud, make it something you'd be proud to display on your business card or on a set of personalized plates. Make your High Concept words that you *will* live by. Challenge your High Concept (after all it is who you are when nobody's looking), improve it with the skills you learned from the second half of the book.

Understand this—you are distinctive! Leave some evidence that you were on this planet! Fill the space! What a gift you are! How wonderful it is to know who you are when nobody's looking! Now go out and share it with the rest of the world!

> "If you see an apple and you leave it lying on the ground, it will spoil. If you pick it up and take a bite, it becomes a part of you forever . . . Everything is on its way to somewhere."
>
> —John Travolta, as George Malley
> in the movie *Phenomenon*

THE AUTHOR AND ILLUSTRATOR

Marc Marsan

Marc is a "marketing mercenary" whose techniques of inventive thinking have helped create successful new products for Gatorade, Disney, Nike, AT&T, Quaker Oats, SC Johnson, Miller Brewing, General Mills, Kimberly Clark and over 200 Fortune 500 companies. In the past six years, Marc has facilitated more than 500 invention sessions and has spoken to thousands of people on the power of innovation and creativity in his "Think Naked" speech series. Marc has been featured in the *National Enquirer*—no, not as an alien baby. He has been an expert guest on *The Montel Williams Show* and on Jack Linkletter's nationally syndicated radio broadcast *Breakthrough Leadership*. In 1998, the Mazda Corporation selected Marc as one of America's top "Out-of-the-Box Thinkers," along with Dennis Rodman, Judge Mills Lane, MTV's Eric Fogel and TV's Mother Love.

Marc has earned several patents, as well as a *Guinness Book of Records* citation for "World's Largest Dance" when he organized 48,000 people to perform the chicken dance in September 1994. He is the father of a ten-year-old son and makes his home in Cincinnati, where he teaches a class on the "Art and Science of Innovation" at the University of Cincinnati Graduate School of Business. Marc is a principal with Synectics, the renowned "think tank" in Cambridge, Massachusetts.

If *Who Are You When Nobody's Looking?* has helped give you new direction in your life, I want to hear from you! Please write me or send me an e-mail with your name, your new High Concept and a personal story about how the book helped you.

> Marc Marsan
> P.O. Box 8293
> Cincinnati, OH 45208
> *or e-mail to* Marsano@aol.com

Gary Kopervas

Gary is the syndicated cartoonist of *Out On a Limb*, which appears in more than 200 newspapers nationwide. He is an award-winning advertising writer for the Sawtooth Group, and a frequent contributor to the well-known cartoon strip *Hagar the Horrible.* He lives in New Jersey and is the father of two boys.